Documentary Credit Law
throughout the world

Annotated legislation from more than 35 countries

Professor Dr Rolf A. Schütze and Dr Gabriele Fontane

The world business organization

Published in December 2001 by

ICC PUBLISHING S.A.
International Chamber of Commerce
The world business organization
38 Cours Albert 1er
75008 Paris, France

ICC Publication No. 633
ISBN 92-842-1298-7

Preface

By Rolf A. Schütze and Gabriele Fontane
Stuttgart/Frankfurt am Main, October 2001

Since their adoption at the 7th Congress of ICC in Vienna in 1933, the Uniform Customs and Practice for Documentary Credits (UCP) have achieved worldwide recognition. The five revisions of the UCP – the most recent of which became effective on 1 January 1994 – have regularly brought UCP into line with the constantly changing commercial environment and the requirements of banking practice. At all times the UCP have remained modern and up-to-date rules.

Today's broad international acknowledgement of the UCP has meant that many countries have no specific statutory provisions on documentary credits. Nevertheless, a number of national statutes do govern documentary credits, and it is one of the ambitions of this book to publish a compilation of them for the first time in English.

The UCP can lead the involved parties to believe that there is nothing further to do once they have agreed to apply the rules. Despite the comprehensive nature of the UCP, one of their characteristics is that they remain an incomplete set of rules. They leave various issues to the applicable national law, such as the statute of limitations, *force majeure* and questions concerning the fraudulent use of documentary credits. The first part of this book, an introduction to the subject matter, addresses these issues. The second section contains references to issues of possible dispute in each jurisdiction, in addition to national statutory provisions.

ICC's newsletter, *Documentary Credits Insight (DCI)*, and ICC's subscription website, DC-PRO, contain useful information on the subject. The reports published in *DCI* are referred to in the footnotes of the second part of this book.

The authors thank Pascale Reins and Ron Katz of ICC for their encouragement to write this book and for publishing it as an ICC publication. The authors also thank those colleagues and partners of their firm Thümmel, Schütze & Partners who contributed their international experience.

Contents

Part Two – Country Statutes

Annexes

Part One
General Principles

1. The law of documentary credits

Documentary credits are known and used around the world as an instrument to secure proper payment of cross-border transactions. It may seem surprising that many jurisdictions' statutes do not specifically address documentary credits, although they are undisputedly legal instruments. In western countries, in particular, few statutes exist that deal specifically with them. In these countries, they are governed by general civil and commercial laws.

Since these laws do not always meet the needs of the parties to a documentary credit transaction, trade and banking organizations have developed their own sets of rules, of which the most widespread and internationally acknowledged are the *Uniform Customs and Practice for Documentary Credits* of the International Chamber of Commerce (UCP). The parties to a documentary credit not only apply the UCP in the absence of any statutory provisions, they also generally agree that the UCP shall prevail – even if there is a special law in place that governs documentary credits – or at least that they should apply, as additional rules that supplement their local documentary credit statute. Whether the UCP or national laws prevail depends on the applicable national law and the parties' agreement – if they have the freedom to create their own contract rules.

Even if the parties agree on the application of the UCP, national statutes on documentary credits need to be taken into consideration. Although the UCP are often used as an unmodified set of rules in all parts of the world, there is no uniform interpretation of the rules by practitioners and courts. In addition, UCP do not address all issues that the parties to a documentary credit may be confronted with; therefore, national statutes and jurisprudence are sources of law even if the UCP apply.

2. Codified provisions

2.1 Statutes

Countries whose laws include special provisions on documentary credits are in a minority[1]. The quality of the statutory provisions varies widely, from comprehensive coverage – such as that found in Article 5 of the Uniform Commercial Code of the United States – to much simpler rules that do not contain much more than a reference to the applicability of "the Uniform Customs and Practice for Documentary Credits of the International Chamber of Commerce[2] ".

While certain geographic areas do not recognize any statutory provisions on documentary credits – the only statute on documentary credits in the European Union is included in the Greek Commercial Code – there is an accumulation of special laws on documentary credits in other regions, for example, in South and Latin America or in the Arab-speaking countries.

Some national law rules correspond to provisions of the UCP; others handle issues differently from the UCP, such as the Kuwaiti or Colombian principle of the documentary credit's general revocability.

2.2 Uniform Customs and Practice for Documentary Credits

The most comprehensive codification of rules on documentary credits are the *Uniform Customs and Practice for Documentary Credits* issued by the International Chamber of Commerce. Since their adoption at ICC's 7th congress in 1933, the UCP have been accepted throughout the world of international trade and banking. Today the rules are the acknowledged standard for financial institutions and trade organizations. Banks in the vast majority of countries have declared their formal adherence to the UCP, even though ICC now discourages the use of formal adherence lists[3].

As noted, UCP are not a complete set of rules. They are not meant to rewrite general laws or to set up an internationally applicable law on documentary credits. The UCP 500 aim to codify acknowledged practices and to provide practical assistance to the parties to a documentary credit transaction. They are incomplete when it comes to setting general legal standards regarding how they shall be applied, remedies for unfulfilled transactions, or how they should be interpreted. National laws provide the necessary back up in such cases if the UCP do not offer a solution.

---

[1] See the second part of this book, which includes all known statutes on documentary credits.
[2] See § 14 of Decree No. 6/97 of the President of the Hungarian Federal Reserve Bank.
[3] As to the meaning of such adherence, see section 2.2.3 of this book.

2.2.1 History of the UCP

Since their initial adoption by ICC in 1933, the UCP have been revised five times. The most recent revision became effective on 1 January 1994[4]. The original 1933 version of the UCP was far more rudimentary than today's UCP 500, but nevertheless their adoption and application was of major significance[5]. Their main achievement was to establish harmonized rules for documentary credit transactions and to override diversions in those rules previously set up by national banking associations such as the *clauses et modalités applicable aux ouvertures de crédit documentaire par l'Union Syndicale des Banques de Paris et de la Province* of 14 January 1924, the regulations adopted by the New York Bankers' Commercial Credit Conference of 1920, or the German *Regulativ für das Akkreditivgeschäft der Berliner Stempelvereinigung* of 1 January 1923.

The first version of the UCP[6] was acknowledged and used by banks predominantly in Belgium, France, Germany, Italy, Romania, the Netherlands and Switzerland. As international trade resumed after the Second World War, changing trade practices led to the first revision of the UCP in 1951[7]. After this first revision, the UCP gained more and more international acceptance. However, they were still far from being acknowledged worldwide, since England and the Commonwealth did not recognize them.

In subsequent years, certain Articles of the UCP were interpreted differently from country to country. As a first attempt to resolve differing opinions on interpretation, ICC published a commentary in 1957 and, in 1962, adopted a new revision of the rules. The 1962[8] revision aimed to adjust the UCP to new developments in trade and to create security by a more precise wording of the rules. Like the previous revision, the 1962 revision aimed to increase the rules' international acceptance, which it largely succeeded in doing. The 1962 revision was acknowledged by banks in 178 countries and territories including the countries of the Commonwealth.

---

[4] ICC Publication No. 500.
[5] Regarding earlier developments of ICC see Taylor, *The History of the UCP, 2000 Annual Survey 201.*
[6] ICC Publication No. 69.
[7] ICC Publication No. 151.
[8] ICC Publication No. 222.

As transportation and shipment systems became more sophisticated, a further revision of the UCP was adopted in 1974[9]. New container transport and so-called combined transport called for an update of the rules at that time. New technical standards in transportation and telecommunications led to another revision in 1983[10], which addressed for the first time deferred payment credits.

The most recent revision of the UCP in 1993 was influenced not so much by technical developments as by international changes in trade and shipment documents. It also attempted to make the existing rules easier to use and to eliminate ambiguity. The publication of four *Position Papers of the ICC Banking Commission* soon after the introduction of UCP 500 was meant to further clarify the correct interpretation of various Articles therein.

2.2.2 Application of the UCP

Opinions concerning the application of the UCP range from regarding them as standard contract terms, to considering them to be *lex mercatoria*. Some regard the UCP as codified commercial customs, customary law or as statutes having a *sui generis* character. While standard contract terms require an agreement between the parties that they shall be part of the credit, customary law, commercial customs or a *lex mercatoria* will apply regardless of the parties' express agreement. Thus, an opinion concerning the legal nature of the UCP automatically determines the requirements for their application.

It is doubtful whether the UCP have the quality of customary law or commercial customs. This would require that the UCP be established and practised usage, which is accepted by trade and banking circles as binding rules. The frequent revisions of the UCP – which were called for by the changing environment surrounding documentary credit transactions – indicated that the authors of the UCP desired in part to alter existing customs that were not being widely used and to reflect new practice in ways that were efficient and workable. The UCP have reacted to changing conditions in the market place, and many of the changes introduced by revisions of the UCP did not have a long-standing history at the time they were written into the rules.

---

[9] ICC Publication No. 290.
[10] ICC Publication No. 400.

It is questionable whether the parties regard the UCP as binding provisions that are effective regardless of the parties' agreement. The introduction of the *International Standby Practices* (ISP98)[11] shows that some market participants do not always agree to use the provisions of the UCP as they apply to standby letters of credit, and that they prefer a different set of rules to apply to these transactions.

In many jurisdictions the view prevails that the UCP are a set of standard business conditions and that they become part of the parties' agreement if the parties explicitly so agree, or if their conduct implies that it is the parties' intention that the UCP apply. Some jurisdictions subject standard business conditions to special laws that control, and to a certain extent restrain, their contents. The motivation of these laws is to protect a contracting party who does not have the power to reject a commercially stronger party's pre-drafted business conditions. The UCP are a codification of rules that has been prepared by considering the interests of all parties to documentary credit transactions with the intention of creating universally accepted rules. Thus, their character is different from the provisions that are customarily governed by protective statutes or standard business conditions.

The unique character of the UCP as a system of rules that are accepted and acknowledged by all concerned parties, and that considers multiparty interests and their international effect, does not permit comparison of the UCP with any existing scheme of law or contractual provisions. Thus, they should be regarded as *sui generis* rules.

ICC is right in recommending that the UCP shall only apply if the parties agree on their application. After all, the UCP are rules that are not drafted by a public authority and thus they remain a privately created system of rules that, at some time in the future, might attain the quality of a *lex mercatoria*. Whether the parties have agreed on their application is a question that is not answered by the UCP but by the laws applying to the agreement to open the credit. Therefore, there is no general rule for determining if the UCP apply.

2.2.3 Adherence to the UCP

Since their introduction in 1933, it had become good practice among banks around the world to express their adherence to the UCP. In many countries such adherence was declared on a collective basis by the

---

[11] ICC Publication No. 590.

national banking association. In recent years the meaning of such adherence has become questionable since neither the adherence declared by the individual bank nor the collective adherence declaration by a national banking association has any binding effect on the parties to a credit.

It is tempting to regard the adherence – regardless of whether it is expressed on an individual or a collective basis – as a general agreement of banks to apply the UCP to all of their documentary credits. Although this is the intention of the formal expression of adherence, such a method of adoption might not work in many systems of law. The application of the UCP needs to be agreed by the parties to the documentary credit, i.e. there must be an expression of consent – either by words or in the parties' conduct – that a party wants to apply the UCP, and the other party must recognize and acknowledge this intention. Therefore, reference to the UCP must be included in the credit document itself to constitute an agreement between the parties on the application of the UCP.

2.2.4 Interpretation of the UCP

Since the UCP do not provide for systematic, comprehensive and complete rules for documentary credit transactions, national laws play an important role. This is particularly true for all issues that are intentionally not addressed by the UCP, such as the application of the rules, the legal nature of the relationships between the parties to a documentary credit, the completion of the documentary credit transaction, and the legal nature of the credit itself. None of these issues is governed by the UCP, since this would go beyond the purpose of the rules.

The relationship between the UCP and national laws becomes more diffuse when a case is generally governed by the UCP but when the UCP do not contain express provisions for a specific aspect of such case, or when the meaning of a term used by the UCP is in question. Some authors are of the opinion that there is a hierarchy between the UCP and national laws and that national laws should be applied whenever the UCP are incomplete or when there is a question of interpretation. Such a fallback relationship between national laws and UCP would require that national laws be capable of providing solutions to any issues open to interpretation.

It is evident that this position is dubious where national statutes do not contain any specific provisions on documentary credits and do not even recognize documentary credits as a legal concept. In such a case, the general provisions of the applicable law must be applied, and these might not be in accord with the UCP, and could even disregard concepts found in the rules. In addition, the domestic scope of national statutes automatically contradicts the international ambitions of the UCP. While the UCP aim to harmonize worldwide trade practices and aim to safeguard the interests of the international trade and banking community, national laws vary from country to country. The application of national laws to issues not expressly addressed by the UCP can result in a de-internationalization of the rules and ultimately conflict with their purpose.

The application of national laws and doctrines needs to be handled carefully. If the UCP generally address an issue in question but do not provide for an explicit solution to a particular aspect of it, there is also the option of considering whether a solution can be found in a general rule contained in the UCP. An interpretation of the UCP in accordance with their aims and evaluations is generally preferable[12].

It can be argued that only if the UCP do not provide any assistance for a conclusive interpretation should national laws and national doctrines apply. If the meaning of a specific term used in the UCP is in question, it will often be unavoidable to interpret such a term in accordance with concepts of national law. This is particularly true if such term is of a legal nature, such as "Act of God" in Article 17 of UCP 500[13]. Especially where applicable laws recognize and use legal terminology also used in the UCP, such terminology is likely to be interpreted in accordance with national law.

An exception to this may occur if the UCP obviously use an expression in a different context from how it is used in national law, or if an expression in UCP describes a concept different from the one used in

---

[12] Schinnerer/Avancini, *Bankverträge*, vol. III, 3rd edition, Vienna 1976, p. 8; Bontoux, *La pratique du crédit documentaire: Quelques problemes particulaires, Hommage à Frederique Eisemann, liber amicorum*, Paris 1978, p. 162; Slongo, *Die Zahlung unter Vorbehalt im Akkreditiv-Geschäft*, Zurich 1980, p. 62; Jack, *Documentary Credits*, 2nd edition, London, Dublin, Edinburgh 1993, n. 1.27; de Rooy, *Documentary Credits*, Antwerp, Boston, London, Frankfurt 1984, p. 16; Ulrich, *Rechtsprobleme des Dokumentenakkreditivs*, Zurich 1989, p. 58.

[13] Hedley/Hedley, *Bills of Exchange and Bankers' Documentary Credits*, 4th edition, London, Hong Kong 2001, p. 364.

such laws, such as the meaning ascribed to general expressions concerning dates for shipment in Article 46 of UCP 500, or the date terminology included in Article 47. The UCP themselves provide for definitions of the terms referred to in these Articles and no assistance of national laws is necessary to interpret them.

3. Types of credits

There are various features that can be used to classify commercial credits, such as their function, payment mechanism, documentary requirements, time or certainty of enforcement. The following is a general categorization that distinguishes between the types of credits in accordance with the conditions and requirements that trigger the bank's payment obligation.

3.1 Documentary credit/cash credit

Payment under a documentary credit is made only if the beneficiary presents documents that comply with the terms of the credit document. The UCP themselves contain a definition of the documentary credit in Article 2. The description of the documents that need to be presented for payment is subject to the agreement between the parties to the underlying transaction.

By describing the documents and the obligation of the paying bank to examine the documents with reasonable care and only to make payment if the documents on their face comply with the terms of the credit, the applicant and the beneficiary both achieve a high degree of security: first, to receive payment for the goods, and second, that payment will only be made if the goods are on their way to the applicant. The documentary credit helps the parties overcome their geographic distance and turns their performances into concurrent conditions – even though the physical trade transaction could never be completed as such.

The requirement to present documents distinguishes the documentary credit from the simple cash credit. This latter type of credit is rarely used today since it lacks the security that is provided by a documentary credit. Payment on a cash credit is to be made upon presentation of the credit and proof of the beneficiary's identity. The cash credit is therefore nothing more than a legitimizing document.

3.2 Standby letter of credit[14]

The standby letter of credit was also introduced by Anglo-American banks and is a result of the earlier prohibition to issue guarantees[15] imposed on American banks. It is therefore not surprising that the standby letter of credit has the function and commercial effect of a guarantee. Objections resulting from the underlying transaction are not permitted, and consequently the standby letter of credit has many of the characteristics of a first demand guarantee.

The standby letter of credit and the documentary credit differ in the types of documents that need to be presented for payment. For payment under a standby letter of credit the beneficiary needs to provide a payment demand stating that the applicant has not met his obligations under the secured transaction and possibly some supporting documents to substantiate the claim.

3.3 Revocable and irrevocable credit

The revocable credit is distinct from the irrevocable credit in that it is less certain that the issuing bank will make payment under the credit. Sub-Article 8(a) of UCP 500 permits the issuing bank to amend or cancel a revocable credit at any moment without prior notice to the beneficiary. In some jurisdictions the revocable credit is referred to as a "simple credit"[16].

The revocable and the irrevocable credit both constitute binding payment promises of the issuing bank. However, the payment promise of the bank issuing a revocable credit is always subject to modification or cancellation without prior approval. The commercial importance of the revocable credit is considerably less than that of the irrevocable credit, because of its restricted certainty of payment.

In the UCP revisions of 1974 and 1983, a credit was deemed revocable unless expressly denominated as irrevocable. Documentary credit practitioners often made the criticism that this rule did not correspond to the commercial relevance of irrevocable credits and the needs of the practice. ICC took this criticism into consideration in drafting the UCP 500 and changed the rule to its opposite: under UCP 500, unless otherwise provided, a credit is irrevocable.

---

[14] see Spjut, *Standby Letters of Credit, 2000 Annual Survey 187*, commenting on the ISP98.
[15] Ellinger/Barry, *Standby Letters of Credit*, IBL 1978, 605; Richter, *Standby letter of credit*, Zurich 1990, p. 48.
[16] Balossini, *Norme ed Usi Uniformi Relativi ai Crediti Documentari*, 4th edition, Milano 1988, p. 83.

The revocability or irrevocability of a credit is addressed in the majority of the country statutes on documentary credits, indicating the considerable importance attached to this issue. Most statutes treat documentary credits as irrevocable if there is no indication to the contrary. Nevertheless, there are also certain countries that provide for a general revocability[17].

The irrevocable credit constitutes a definite payment undertaking by the issuing bank which may not be altered or cancelled at a later time without the consent of the beneficiary and confirming bank, if any. The obligations of the bank issuing or confirming an irrevocable credit are described in Article 9 of UCP 500.

A revocable credit cannot be confirmed by a nominated bank. In the exceptional and somewhat unusual case that an nominated bank confirms the revocable credit in error, the confirmation only applies to the obligation of the issuing bank. The confirmation is nothing more than the assumption of the issuing bank's obligation. The confirmation does not make the credit irrevocable. Thus, the nominated bank may – after becoming aware of its error – claim that it is not bound to its confirmation. Some doctrinal writers also support the view that the bank confirming a revocable credit may subsequently cancel its undertaking[18].

3.4 Confirmed documentary credit

The confirmation of a documentary credit by an nominated bank creates an independent obligation of such nominated bank that exists in addition to the obligation of the issuing bank. In other words, the confirmation of the credit multiplies the payment claim of the beneficiary. The obligation of the confirming bank is independent from the obligation of the issuing bank. Thus, the claims of the beneficiary may be subject to different jurisdictions, different objections by the bank or different statutes of limitations. Nevertheless, the obligations of both banks are identical. It is acknowledged that, as debtors, the issuing and confirming bank are jointly and severally liable to the beneficiary[19].

Certain countries (such as China or Iran) generally have not permitted local banks to confirm documentary credits. In these countries, banks have developed their own concepts of providing a certain degree of comfort

---

[17] Such as Bolivia, Oman or Russia.
[18] e.g. Sarna, *Letters of Credit*, 3rd edition, Ontario 1992, p. 1–10.
[19] Raith, *Das Recht des Dokumentenakkreditivs in den USA und Deutschland*, Bonn 1985, p. 172; Schmidt-Dencker, *Die Korrespondenzbank im Außenhandel*, Hamburg 1980, p. 10.

without confirming credits. Such banks often state that they will "protect" the beneficiary's payment claim. The commercial effect of such a protection clause corresponds to a confirmation of the credit[20].

3.5 Revolving credit

The revolving credit allows the beneficiary to make several drawings under the credit up to a maximum amount. It revolves by value upon a given event on a cumulative or non-cumulative basis, either automatically or non-automatically. Typically, the revolving credit is used if the applicant and the beneficiary are parties to an ongoing trade relationship that involves repeated payments – such as a franchise or distributor agreement.

3.6 Back-to-back credit

The back-to-back credit is a true documentary credit which is predominately used if a non-transferable credit is issued in favour of a beneficiary. The back-to-back credit is issued by the issuing bank or the confirming bank upon request by the beneficiary of the first credit, and the beneficiary of the back-to-back (or second) credit typically is the beneficiary's contract partner from whom he purchases the goods that are sold to the applicant of the first credit. Often the first credit is used to secure the bank that issues the second credit. Both credits are independent of each other. However, they need to be well adjusted and it is essential to ensure that the documents that need to be presented for payment under the second credit can also be used for the first credit[21].

3.7 Deferred payment credit

In contrast to the sight payment credit, a deferred payment credit is payable at an agreed time after the presentation of documents. The purpose of the deferred payment credit is to enable the applicant to refinance the credit's amount by selling or otherwise making use of the purchased goods. Due to the lack of time between the presentation of goods and the payment date, the deferred payment credit is the only type of credit suitable for a forfaiting transaction.

Although the deferred payment credit is payable only at a stipulated time after the presentation of documents, it is not uncommon that banks will make payment to the beneficiary prior to the credit's payment date. The nature of a premature payment under a deferred payment credit is disputed.

---

[20] Schütze, *Das Dokumentenakkreditiv im internationalen Handelsverkehr*, 5th edition, Heidelberg 1999, n. 59.
[21] Sarna, *Letters of Credit*, 3rd edition, Ontario 1992, p. 1–16.

Some courts and commentators treat the premature payment as an anticipatory payment under the credit that fulfils the obligation of the bank[22]. Others regard it, not as performance under the credit, but as a loan to the beneficiary[23]. If the payment is treated as a loan, the beneficiary's claim under the credit is sustained. At the credit's payment date, the bank's obligation under the credit will be set off against the bank's claim for repayment of the loan. The difference between this controversial treatment of a premature payment is crucial.

The nominated bank is entitled to reimbursement from the issuing bank upon the credit's payment date. This means that the interim time between payment to the beneficiary and reimbursement increases the risk of being unable to seek recovery from the beneficiary if the issuing bank rejects the documents as not compliant.

If this payment is regarded as a loan, the bank remains bound to its obligation under the credit. If the beneficiary becomes insolvent, or if his rights under the credit are seized by one of his creditors in the interim period between making the payment and the credit's payment date, the bank will be unable to claim that payment has already been made. Instead, the bank will have to again pay the creditor or the beneficiary's bankrupt estate.

Another method of delaying payment under a documentary credit is to use an acceptance credit. Under an acceptance credit the bank accepts drafts drawn by the beneficiary that are payable, not at sight, but at an agreed point of time in the future.

3.8 Red clause/green clause

A red clause credit permits the bank to pay advances to the beneficiary without presentation of documents. The red clause L/C was developed for the Australian Wool market. It allowed the sheep farmers to pay for the labour in shearing the sheep before the shipment of the finished product. The beneficiary would be able to claim up to 80% of the value in advance against an undertaking from the seller to ship the goods within the timeframe stated in the credit. This type of credit enables the beneficiary either to auction goods or to make test purchases of them from the manufacturer[24].

---

[22] Swiss Federal Court BGE II, 152; Supreme Court of Frankfurt am Main WM 1981, 445.

[23] German Federal Supreme Court WM 1987, 977; Plagemann, *Arrestierung des Auszahlungsanspruches aus einem deferred payment-Akkreditiv*, RIW 1987, 27.

[24] Bertrand, *Etude sur la red clause*, Rev. de la Banque 1955, 90; Lombardini, *Droit et Pratique du Crédit Documentaire*, Zurich 1994, p. 19; Slongo, *Die Zahlung unter Vorbehalt im Akkreditivgeschäft*, Zurich 1980, p. 102.

The unpaid balance of the credit will only be paid to the beneficiary upon presentation of compliant documents.

A green clause credit requires that the goods that are paid by the documentary credit be stored in the name of the issuing bank until they are sold by way of a release by the issuing bank.

The name of these credits is taken from the colour of the ink originally used on the credit document for highlighting the respective special obligations of the parties.

4. Form and contents of the documentary credit

4.1 General

The UCP do not expressly require any specific form or format of documentary credits. However, Article 1 uses the term "text" which implies that a credit shall be opened in writing. Accordingly, the prevailing jurisprudence requires that a credit be opened in writing[25]. ICC has developed standard forms for issuing documentary credits, and these are used by banks, with slight modifications[26].

The minimum contents of a credit include the name of the beneficiary, applicant, expiry date, amount of the credit, place of presentation of the documents, the promise to make payment if the terms of the credit are complied with, provisions concerning the means of honouring the credit, and specification of the documents.

4.2 Expiry date

The expiry date, which must be included in the credit according to Article 42 of UCP 500, is the deadline for presentation of documents. It is not to be confused with a statute of limitations. Once the compliant documents have been timely presented, the beneficiary's payment claim is not time barred by the expiry date[27]. If the credit does not provide for an expiry date, it is invalid.

In addition to the expiry date, sub-Article 43(a) of UCP 500 provides that the credit should stipulate a specific period of time after the shipment of the goods during which documents should be presented. This period may reduce but not extend the validity period of the credit. In the absence of

---

[25] Balossini, *Norme ed Usini Uniformi Relativi ai Crediti Documentari*, 4th edition 1988, p. 78; Kozolchyk, *Letters of Credit*, 1979, p. 92 with further references.

[26] See appendices.

[27] As to the statute of limitations see section 14.

such a period, banks will refuse to take up documents that are presented 21 days after the date of shipment or after the expiry date of the credit, whichever is the earlier.

Documentary credit transactions do not permit grace periods. If the expiry date has passed and the documents have not been presented on or prior to that date, or prior to the expiration of the presentation period, the obligations under the credit lapse. The only exception to these rigid deadlines can be found in Article 44 of UCP 500, which provides that the expiry date is extended to the next working day if it falls on a date on which banks are closed for reasons other than those referred to in Article 17. In other words, the expiry date is extended if it falls on a Saturday, Sunday (if the bank in question is not open on these days) or on a national bank holiday. No other reasons can extend the life of the credit.

4.3 Place of payment

The stipulation of a place of presentation does not obligate the beneficiary to present the documents at that specified place. The beneficiary has a choice of whether to use the stipulated place of presentation or to present the documents to the issuing bank.

In principle, all parties to the credit are bound to stipulate their agreement on the place of presentation. However, such a stipulation is made only for the convenience of, and in favour of, the beneficiary. Consequently, the beneficiary may waive his right to present the documents at the place of presentation.

The absence of a stipulation as to a place of presentation does not invalidate the credit. Documents are then to be presented at the issuing bank or any other bank at which the credit is available for negotiation or payment.

4.4 Amount

The credit must specify the amount to be paid according to the underlying transaction and the applicable currency. When the applicant does not know the final sum to be paid, Article 39 of UCP 500 allows for a degree of flexibility. By adding expressions such as "approximately", "about" or "circa", the applicant can avoid difficulties if the ultimate purchase price varies from the expected price, e.g. due to discrepancies in the weight of the goods. The expressions "approximately", "about" or "circa" and the like are construed to allow differences in the amount of +/- 10%.

4.5 Beneficiary

In earlier documentary credit practice, banks at times agreed to issue credits without specifying the beneficiary in order to facilitate the credit's transfer and compliance. Today such credits are rarely found, and standard bank forms require the name of the beneficiary.

The beneficiary must be clearly specified; discrepancies between the beneficiary's name and how he or she is referred to in the credit can permit banks to refuse to honour the credit. To avoid any doubts, it often is recommended that the beneficiary's address be included in the credit, facilitating identification.

5. Obligations under the credit

5.1 Relationship between applicant and beneficiary

If the parties to a trade transaction agree that payment shall be made by documentary credit, the purchaser will instruct his or her bank to issue the credit in favour of the beneficiary. This will not release the applicant from his payment obligation to the beneficiary, since this obligation is satisfied only upon payment of the documentary credit.

The agreement that payment shall be made by a documentary credit obligates the beneficiary to use the credit and to refrain from demanding payment directly from the applicant. If the credit expires unused, the beneficiary's payment claim against the applicant remains and can be enforced. However, the applicant may set off against payment the damages resulting from losses that he may have suffered due to the beneficiary's failure to use the credit.

5.2 Relationship between applicant and issuing bank

The applicant's request to his bank to issue a credit is deemed to be an offer to conclude the credit agreement, which is confirmed if the bank agrees to issue the credit. In practice, especially in long-term customer relationships, banks often issue the credit immediately and subsequently inform the applicant by forwarding a copy of the credit to him. In these cases, the bank's acceptance to open the credit is expressed tacitly.

The bank's main obligations are to open the credit and to honour it if compliant documents are presented by the beneficiary. The applicant is obligated to reimburse the credit amount to the bank if the credit is honoured in compliance with its terms, to pay the bank a commission, and to compensate its expenses incurred in opening and handling the credit. Expenses subject to compensation by the applicant include legal fees incurred in connection with the enforcement of reimbursement claims against the applicant, regardless of whether the bank succeeds or fails to obtain a court order against him[28].

Sometimes banks demand that the applicant advance the amount of the credit or deposit it in an account with the bank. If the bank honours the credit, it simply debits the amount from the applicant's account.

5.3 Relationship between issuing bank and beneficiary

The bank's obligation to the beneficiary arises once the beneficiary obtains knowledge of the credit. No express acceptance by the beneficiary is necessary to constitute the bank's payment obligation. If the credit's contents are not in compliance with the agreement between the beneficiary and the applicant, the beneficiary must seek an amendment to the credit or reject the credit promptly. The beneficiary is not entitled to request that the bank correct the credit's contents, since the bank is only bound to the instructions received from the applicant.

The beneficiary has a right against the applicant, however, to demand the issuance of a credit that is in compliance with the agreed terms. If the credit is not in conformity with his agreement with the applicant, and if he does not reject it, he is deemed to have accepted it, even if it has been amended by the applicant.

5.4 Relationship between advising bank/nominated bank and beneficiary/applicant

Correspondent banks[29] are often involved in a documentary credit transaction either as an advising bank, a nominated bank or a confirming bank. An advising bank's involvement is of a purely technical nature. When the issuing bank does not have a presence in the country of the beneficiary's domicile, it uses a correspondent bank to advise the beneficiary of the issuance of the credit.

---

[28] Avancini/Iro/Koziol, *Österreichisches Bankvertragsrecht*, vol. II, 1993, n. 4/67; German Federal Supreme Court, WM 1998, 1769; Schütze/Fontane, *DCI,* vol. 4/4, p. 21.

[29] This term is not used in the UCP. The UCP exclusively refer to a correspondent bank either as advising bank, nominated bank or confirming bank depending on such bank's function in the credit transaction.

The advising bank is only bound to the agreement with the issuing bank. There are no direct contractual ties to the applicant and the beneficiary. The advising of the credit imposes only quasi-contractual duties on the advising bank – such as the duty to check the apparent authenticity of the credit with reasonable care as provided for in Article 7 of UCP 500. The same is true for the relationship between the beneficiary and the nominated bank, which only imposes certain quasi-contractual duties, such as the duty to take up and forward compliant documents to the issuing bank. There are no direct engagements between the applicant and nominated banks.

5.5 Relationship between confirming bank and beneficiary

The confirming bank undertakes direct contractual obligations to the beneficiary. Its obligations are identical to those of the issuing bank, and the confirmation of the credit creates an obligation in addition to that of the issuing bank. The issuing bank and the confirming bank are liable to the beneficiary as joint and several creditors.

5.6 Legal qualification of relationships

The legal status of the credit opening agreement between the issuing bank and the applicant, and all other relationships created under the documentary credit, depend on the law applicable to those relationships. Consequently, the examination of any issues pertaining to them, such as their validity, default by one party or remedies of default, require a prior determination of the applicable law.

6. Conflict of laws

6.1 Determination of applicable law

A documentary credit triggers a number of questions concerning what should be the applicable law. The UCP do not provide any assistance in this respect since they do not deal with conflict of laws; however, the parties could easily overcome any uncertainty by including a choice of law clause in the credit document. Although such clauses have been recommended[30], the parties often ignore this advice, since they are unaware of its significance.

---

[30] Teoh Oon Teong, *Letters of Credit: A Conflict of Laws Perspective*, 2 Singapore Acadamy of Law Journal (1990), 51; Schärrer, *Die Rechtsstellung des Begünstigten im Dokumenten-Akkreditiv*, 1980, p. 41; Gozlan, *International Letters of Credit*, 2nd edition 1999, p. 36; Lombardini, *Droit et pratique du crédit documentaire*, 1994, p. 190; Allen/Pollack, *Letters of Credit – an Underappreciated Financial Vehicle*, Festschrift für Martin Peltzer, 2001, p. 5.

Clearly, the determination of the applicable law is a precondition for deciding any legal issue pertaining to the credit and can be crucial to the outcome of a dispute arising between the parties. In the absence of a choice of law clause, a court must determine the applicable law, taking into account the relationship of the parties disputing an issue arising from the credit. On rare occasions, all relationships pertaining to a documentary credit will be governed by the laws of the same jurisdiction. Failing that, the different relationships will each be subject to a separate determination of the applicable law[31]. In some cases, the relationship between the applicant and the beneficiary, the issuing bank and the beneficiary and the applicant and the issuing bank may each be governed by the laws of a different jurisdiction.

It is acknowledged as a general principle that the independence of the documentary credit from the underlying trade transaction also influences applicable laws. Because of this independence, a choice of law agreement between the parties to the trade transaction will not apply to the documentary credit[32].

6.2 Relationship between applicant and issuing bank

In general, the applicable law of a documentary credit transaction should be determined by the place where the obligations arising under the credit have "their closest and most real connection"[33].

In most cases the law applying to the relationship between the applicant and the issuing bank will not cause difficulties, since typically the applicant will elect a bank domiciled in his own country. Nevertheless, there have been prominent cases where the purchaser was forced to mandate a foreign bank to issue the credit in order to increase its value[34]. The application of the general rule that the governing law is to be determined by looking at the closest and most real connection of each contract results in the inter-nationally acknowledged conclusion that the law governing the relationship between the applicant and the issuing bank is the law of the issuing bank's domicile[35].

---

[31] Lin, *Cross-Border Implications of Standby Credits*, 2000 Annual Survey 133.

[32] Attock Cement Co. Ltd v. Romanian Bank for Foreign Trade cited by Ellinger JBusL 1990, 58; see also de Rooy, *Documentary Credits*, 1984, p. 17; Todd, *Bills of Lading and Bankers' Documentary Credits*, 3rd edition, 1998, p. 295; Schärrer, *Die Rechtstellung des Begünstigten im Dokumenten-Akkreditiv*, Berne 1980, p. 65.

[33] Sinotani Pacific Pte Ltd v. Agricultural Bank of China, 2000 Annual Survey 365.

[34] See the case reported on by Ellinger in *JBusL* 1994, 33.

[35] Kaya, *Die Grenzen der Einwendungen der Bank gegen den Zahlungsanspruch des Begünstigten aus einem unwiderruflichen Akkreditiv*, 2000, p. 132; Lin, *Cross-Border Implications of Standby Credits*, 2000 Annual Survey 136.

6.3 Relationship between issuing bank and beneficiary

It is also internationally acknowledged that the relationship between the issuing bank and the beneficiary is more closely connected to the location of the issuing bank and that the laws of the issuing bank's location should therefore be applied. It is highly disputed whether the appointment of a correspondent bank has an impact on the law governing the beneficiary's claim to honour the credit.

In civil law jurisdictions, the prevailing view is that the appointment of an advising bank does not affect the law applying to the relationship between the beneficiary and the issuing bank. This is the case because the performance of the advising bank is regarded as a purely technical service, and does not create a closer connection to its home country than to the home country of the issuing bank[36].

The appointment of a nominated bank is treated more delicately. Courts and civil law authors disagree as to whether the appointment of such an agent creates a closer and more intense connection to the laws of the country of the nominated bank's location rather than the country of the issuing bank. Some courts and legal writers see the appointment of a nominated bank as a relocation of the credit's place of performance to the nominated bank's domicile, and regard this as the determining factor deciding the applicable law.

While courts in civil law jurisdictions deny any impact on the applicable law if an advising bank is appointed – and it is arguable whether the appointment of a nominated bank affects the applicable law – in both cases courts in common law countries often have expressed the view that the appointment of a correspondent bank subjects the documentary credit to the laws of the place of that correspondent bank. In European Asian Bank AG v. Punjab & Sind Bank[37] the court applied the laws of Singapore, although the only party located in Singapore was the advising bank. The same principle was applied in Offshore International SA v. Banco Central SA[38] where the court decided that the seat of the advising bank in New York created the closest and most real relation to the documentary credit[39].

---

[36] State Supreme Court of Frankfurt am Main, WuB I H 2. – 1.92; Gutzwiller, *Bemerkungen zum Verhältnis zwischen Akkreditivbank and Korrespondenzbank*, SchweizAG 1984, 159.
[37] [1981] 2 Ll. Rep. 651 (657).
[38] [1976] 3 All ER 749 (751).
[39] See also Agritrade International Pte Ltd v. Industrial and Commercial Bank of China, [1998] 3 S.L.R abstracted at 2000 Annual Survey 284; Sinotani Pacific Pte Ltd v. Agricultural Bank of China, 2000 Annual Survey 365.

The international view is more uniform if the credit is confirmed by the correspondent bank. Courts in most jurisdictions support the view that a confirmation of the credit triggers the application of the laws of the confirming bank's jurisdiction[40]. Some authors and courts differentiate between the beneficiary's claim against the confirming bank and its claim against the issuing bank and apply the above rule exclusively to the beneficiary's claim against the confirming bank. They contend that with respect to the applicable law[41] that the beneficiary's claim against the issuing bank remains unaffected by the confirmation.

6.4 Relationship between banks

In the relationship between the issuing and correspondent bank the most real and closest relation is determined by the bank that carries out the main performance. Typically, this will be the correspondent bank, since its performance characterizes the agreement, regardless of whether the correspondent bank acts as advising or confirming bank or as nominated bank. If the correspondent bank acts as the advising bank, the main element of the agreement between it and the issuing bank is the advice involved in issuing the credit to the beneficiary. If the correspondent bank is retained as nominated bank, its obligation to take up documents and to honour the credit is the prevailing performance.

The same is true for the relationship between issuing bank and correspondent bank. The fact that the relationship between the issuing bank and nominated bank/confirming bank also constitutes a claim for reimbursement of paid amounts by the correspondent bank cannot create a link to the location of the issuing bank that is closer and more real than the correspondent bank's obligation. The entitlement to reimbursement is of secondary importance; therefore, the location of the correspondent bank determines the applicable law.

7. Using the documentary credit

The beneficiary's rights under the credit are subject to timely presentation of compliant documents to the issuing or confirming bank, or any other bank that is a nominated bank as defined by Article 10 of UCP 500. The risk of the documents

---

[40] Sarna, *Letters of Credit*, 3rd edition 1992, p. 9–6.
[41] Schütze, *Das Dokumentenakkreditiv im internationalen Handelsverkehr*, 5th edition 1999, n. 476; Özdamar, *Rechtsfragen des Dokumentenakkreditivs in Gestalt seiner Regelung nach den ERA (Revision 1983)*, 1996, p. 190.

being lost after their dispatch by the beneficiary is borne by the beneficiary. If the beneficiary presents the documents at any other bank – such as an advising bank that is not nominated to honour the credit, or the beneficiary's bank – the documents must be received prior to the expiry date of the credit by one of the banks referred to under Article 10 of UCP 500.

The presentation of the documents to a bank other than the issuing, confirming or nominated bank does not cause the beneficiary's payment claim to arise. The beneficiary's risk of lost documents or a late presentation of documents at the issuing, confirming or nominated bank remains, unless the issuing bank expressly instructs the beneficiary to present documents at any other place. In the latter case, the issuing bank may not invoke any claims based on its instructions regarding the presentation of documents, and the beneficiary has met the requirements to enforce his claim to honour the credit[42].

7.1 Examination of documents

The standard for banks' examination of documents is based on the principle set forth in Article 4 of UCP 500. Since banks do not deal with the underlying transaction – but exclusively with documents – banks, when examining documents, are not required to investigate any aspect of the underlying transaction. Nevertheless, banks may consider the underlying transaction in their interpretation of the credit. The doctrines of autonomy and strict compliance set limits to interpretation but in no way prohibit it.

If aspects of the underlying transaction are considered when interpreting the credit, these must be taken from the credit document[43]. If they are not reflected in the credit document they will be disregarded, since to consider them requires a bank to examine circumstances outside the credit, and such examination would violate the cardinal principles of documentary credit transactions.

Article 13 of UCP 500 says that documents have to be examined with "reasonable care". This means the reasonable care of a banker, not of an expert in the business of the underlying transaction, nor one who specializes in the kind of goods or services paid for by the credit[44]. The bank's examination is generally a limited one; therefore, it is sufficient if the documents on their face comply with the credit.

[42] Eisemann/Bontoux/Rowe, *Le crédit documentaire dans le commerce extérieur*, 1985, p. 77; Avancini/Iro/Koziol, *Österreichisches Bankvertragsrecht*, vol. II, 1993, n. 4/103.
[43] Supreme Court of Frankfurt am Main DZWir 1997, 423; Ocean Rig ASA v. Safra National Bank of New York abstracted at 2000 Annual Survey 345.
[44] J.H. Rayner & Co. Ltd v. Hambro's Bank Ltd, supra n. 474, p. 701.

In practice banks often aim to clarify ambiguities in the presented documents and to obtain translations of documents that are presented in languages other than that stipulated in the credit, rather than rejecting the document due to language discrepancies. However, there is no obligation to do so. In particular, banks do not have to identify documents presented in languages other than that stipulated in the credit[45], to determine the validity of company or official stamps, to deal with ambiguities in the documents' reference to the parties, or to consider the legal effect of documents.

7.2 Principle of strict compliance

Documentary credit transactions are judged by the principle of strict compliance. The compliance of the tendered documents with the credit's terms ensures the proper completion of the underlying transaction. Only if the bank strictly adheres to the requirements of the applicant, and only if it makes payment when compliant documents are presented is the security of the documentary credit safeguarded.

Documents are only compliant if they are complete, if they are of the kind described in the credit and if they are without obvious defects. A complete set of documents requires that all the documents referred to in the credit be presented, with the right number of copies of each document as stipulated. Banks do not have to examine whether documents are valid. Nevertheless, they are under a duty to refuse documents that contain obvious irregularities or other obvious formal defects.

In examining whether the documents are in compliance, banks have a very limited discretion with regard to the contents and the type of documents that need to be presented. The classic statement by Lord Sumner[46], "there is no room for documents which are almost the same or which will do just as well" delineates the clear limits of the bank's examination process. Though this standard may seem easy to follow, banks often apply a more pragmatic approach that has resulted in exceptions to the strict compliance doctrine.

Unlike the ISP98, the UCP do not contain any provision concerning the treatment of grammar and typographical errors. However, it is acknowledged that banks may disregard them if they appear to be only mistakes in syntax

---

[45] Supreme Court of Munich, WM 1996, 2335 where the court found that the bank had no obligation to verify whether a document contained an English translation of the beneficiary's name and therefore was entitled to reject the presented document as non-compliant.
[46] Hansson v. Hamel & Horley, [1922] 2 A.C. 46.

or misprints[47]. Discrepancies in numbers, however, never can be disregarded since numbers cannot be subject to interpretation[48]. One acknowledged exception has occurred when discrepancies were so insignificant that they could not affect overall compliance[49]. Another exception has been where synonymous terms are used and the contents of the tendered documents essentially meet the requirements of the credit. At times, however, courts have accepted a bank's rejection of documents containing terms synonymous with rather than identical to those used in the credit[50].

A bank's discretion in examining documents is influenced by the consideration that any discrepancy in the documents could be to their customer's disadvantage. Many banks believe it advisable to take a narrow approach, since the acceptance of discrepant documents can result in personal liabilities for the bank. The applicant is not obligated to reimburse the bank and may demand repayment of any monies deposited with it for payment of the credit.

8. Treatment of non-compliant documents

If non-compliant documents are tendered, banks have an obligation to the applicant to refuse them and to dishonour the credit, though sub-Article 14(c) allows banks to approach the applicant for a waiver of the discrepancies prior to notifying the presenter of the bank's refusal to take up the documents.

The decisions concerning whether or not the documents are in compliance with the terms of the credit and whether the notification of this decision to the beneficiary have to be made within the time stipulated by sub-Article 13(b) of UCP 500, i.e. within a reasonable time, not exceeding seven banking days following the day of receipt of the documents.

The seven-day deadline was first introduced in UCP 500. Older versions of the UCP only required a "reasonable" period of time for the examination of documents.

---

[47] Ocean Rig ASA v. Safra National Bank of New York abstracted at 2000 Annual Survey 345; Gook Country Estates Ltd v. Toronto Dominion Bank, 2000 B.C.D. Civ. J. 3809 (typographical error in address); E&H Partners v. Broadway National Bank, 96 Civ. 7098 (RLC) 1998 (error in postal code); Spjut, Standby Letters of Credit, 2000 Annual Survey 191; Schütze, Das Dokumentenakkreditv im internationalen Handelsverkehr, 5th edition 1999, n. 390 with further references.
[48] German Federal Supreme Court WM 1958, 587.
[49] This exception often is referred to as the de minimis exception.
[50] Bank of Italy v. Merchants National Bank, 121 Wash. 476 (1922) (raisins instead of dried grapes); J.H. Rayner & Co. Ltd v. Hambro's Bank Ltd, Supra n. 474, p. 701 (machine-shelled groundnut kernels instead of Coromandel groundnuts); Courtaulds North America Inc. v. North Carolina National Bank, 528 F.2d 802 (4th Cir. 1975) (imported acrylic yarn instead of 100% acrylic yarn).

The meaning of "reasonable" was subject to intense discussion and the opinions thereon ranged from three- and four-day periods to several weeks[51].

Today there is no doubt that to avoid personal liability a bank, if it judges the documents to be not compliant, is compelled to refuse documents within the seven-day period. Nevertheless, the debate on the definition of a "reasonable time" for the examination of documents has not abated, since sub-Article 13(b) of UCP 500 does not mean that a bank is always permitted to use the full seven days. The standard for the examination of documents is still "a reasonable time", which can be much shorter than seven banking days depending on several factors, including the number, length and complexity of the documents, whether there are obvious discrepancies that can be determined at once, etc.[52].

If the bank refuses to take up non-compliant documents prior to the credit's expiry date, the beneficiary may remedy the defect in the documents and present them again. The examination of the documents in a "reasonable time", rather than for the full seven banking days, is therefore of utmost importance to the beneficiary.

Sub-Article 14(d) of UCP 500 determines how the bank's decision to refuse the tendered documents is to be communicated to the presenter. The reasons for dishonour must be specified in the notice to the presenter.

In addition, the bank shall include in its notice whether it holds non-compliant documents at the disposal of the presenter or returns them to the presenter.

Sub-Article 14(d) does not provide any rules for the calculation of the seven-day period, since the purpose of this period is to ensure that the presenter can count on the fact that, whether or not the bank accepts the presented documents as compliant, he must receive the bank's notice of refusal within the seven days. National methods of calculation, such as the concept that the dispatch of notice is sufficient to meet a deadline, are not relevant.

---

[51] Cour d'Appel de Paris, Droit Maritime Français 1986, 93 (deeming 8 banking days as reasonable); Supreme Court of Hong Kong re Hing Yip Fat Co. Ltd v. Daiwa Bank Ltd, (1991) 2 HKLR 35 (deeming 5 calendar days as reasonable); Bankers Trust Company v. State Bank of India, IFL Rev 1991, 49 (deeming 8 calendar days as not reasonable); Bank Melli Iran v. Barclays Bank (1951) 2 Ll. Rep. 367 ("six weeks can be reasonable"); Dekker, *Case Studies on Documentary Credits*, 1989, ICC Publication No. 459, p. 56 (case no. 50); Ellinger, *Reasonable Time for Examination of Documents*, (1985), JBusL 408; Todd, *A Reasonable Time to Inspect Documents: The Royan, International Banking Law*, vol. 8, 1990, p. 179.

[52] Lombardini, *Droit et pratique du crédit documentaire*, 1994, p. 153; Vorpeil, *Prüfungszeitraum beim Dokumentenakkreditiv ("reasonable time")*, RIW 1993, 15.

Failure of the bank to give notice to the beneficiary in accordance with the requirements of Article 14 of UCP 500 precludes the bank from dishonouring the credit. This is equally true of failure to meet the seven-day deadline and to inform the beneficiaries of the discrepancies found in the documents[53].

9. Fraud

As noted, banks deal exclusively with documents and disregard the merits of the underlying transaction. If the documents are in compliance with the credit, banks are entitled and obligated to honour the credit. This general rule does not apply where the use of the credit is evidently fraudulent. In such case the bank is entitled – and under certain circumstances is under an obligation to the applicant – to dishonour the credit.

The UCP do not expressly address issues of fraud. Article 15 of UCP states that banks do not accept any liabilities for cases of fraud. However, it does not define fraud or explain the consequences if there is fraud in a documentary credit transaction. There are varying standards in each jurisdiction concerning the bank's right and obligation to refuse payment in such cases. Since the principles of strict compliance and autonomy of the credit prevail, the right and obligation to refuse payment due to a misuse of the credit can only arise in exceptional cases. The immorality of the underlying transaction or simple defects in it, such as the delivery of goods of an inferior quality, are not sufficient reasons to dishonour the credit[54]. If they were, banks would become involved in the underlying transaction and violate the cardinal principles of Article 3 of UCP 500.

Defects in the relationship between the applicant and the beneficiary have to be sufficiently serious to render payment under the credit intolerable[55]. Courts in different jurisdictions regard this threshold to be exceeded if the performance of the beneficiary clearly does not correspond with the performance owed under the underlying transaction, such as in case of a delivery of worthless material instead of the contractual goods[56], or no delivery at all. In such cases, the beneficiary deliberately misuses the credit and thereby commits an act of fraud[57].

---

[53] Hamilton Bank NA v. Kooknun Bank, 98 Civ. 2162 abstracted at 2000 Annual Survey 323.
[54] Cherubino Valsangiacomo SA v. American Juice Imports, Inc., Tex. App. LEXIS 375 abstracted at 2000 Annual Survey 299.
[55] Leslie v. Lloyds of London, 85 F.3d 625 (5th Cir. 1996).
[56] Steijn v. Henri Schoeder Banking Corporation, 31 N.Y.S. 2d 364.
[57] Barclays Bank of Canada v. Canadian Commercial Bank, 173 D.L.R. 309 abstracted at 2000 Annual Survey 292.

In instances of evident bad faith, the bank no longer has an obligation to the beneficiary to honour the credit, even if the beneficiary presents compliant documents. The principles of strict compliance and autonomy of the credit are not meant to protect a beneficiary who acts fraudulently[58].

If the use of the credit is an abuse by the beneficiary of his rights, a second question arises as to how the abuse must be brought to the bank's attention. It is questionable whether a bank's being informed of a misuse of the credit by its customer is sufficient. By using a documentary credit, the parties intend to avoid any influence by the buyer on the payment of the purchase price once the goods or services owed by the seller are no longer under the seller's control.

The bank may not rely on the applicant's simple allegations[59]; rather it has to obtain actual and definite knowledge of the beneficiary's fraud. Therefore, the bank is only entitled to refuse payment if there is *prima facie* evidence of fraud. In such a case the bank is not only entitled, but is also under a duty to the applicant, to deny payment of the credit. The standards for such *prima facie* evidence are very high, and in practice banks will not refuse to honour a credit unless the applicant's allegations are confirmed by a court order and the court prohibits the bank to honour the credit.

10. Injunctive relief

If the applicant finds that there is fraud in the transaction, the issuing bank may not always follow his instruction to dishonour the credit. Dishonouring a credit can trigger claims for damages by the beneficiary and could impair the bank's reputation.

If the bank refuses to dishonour a credit upon the applicant's request, the applicant has to seek judicial assistance through an injunction. However, the use of injunctive restraining orders diminishes the certainty of a payment under a credit, and for this reason courts should be – and in most jurisdictions are – reluctant to grant injunctive relief[60]. Requirements vary from one jurisdiction to another with regard to the evidence sufficient to warrant such relief; there is no uniform international treatment of applications for injunctions.

---

[58] Sztejn v. J. Henry Schoeder Banking Corporation, 31 N.Y.S. 2d 364.
[59] Royal Bank of Scotland v. Holmes [1999] S.L.T. 563.
[60] In some countries courts take a rather liberal view on injunction prohibiting payment under a documentary credits. As a consequence the standing of banks in those countries as issuing or confirming banks has declined.

Requests for restraining orders prohibiting the beneficiary from presenting documents cause material risks and practical difficulties and are therefore not preferable. The purpose of an injunction is to provide the applicant with temporary protection against irreparable injury. If an injunction is handed down that prohibits the beneficiary from presenting documents, the credit may expire while the injunction is in effect. In such a case, the injunction would vest the applicant with disproportionate rights, since instead of providing temporary protection, it would create a permanent situation in which the beneficiary can no longer use the credit.

In addition, the injunction may not always result in the desired protection, since it is addressed only to the beneficiary. The beneficiary might be able to transfer the credit to a *bona fide* acting second beneficiary who is not subject to the injunction and who may present the documents to the bank[61].

Therefore, applying for an injunction that prohibits the beneficiary from receiving payment of the credit is not a preferred option. Depending on the *lex fori*, this might require an injunctive order to be served on the beneficiary prior to the order becoming effective. This can create practical difficulties, depending on the beneficiary's domicile.

The preferable method of preventing payment to the beneficiary is to attach his payment claim if the *lex fori* provides that the attachment order becomes effective at the time of service on the bank[62]. Service on the beneficiary then only need be effected a certain period of time after the date of the court order. During the time between service on the bank and on the beneficiary, the credit is blocked.

The treatment of applications for a restraining order against the issuing or the confirming bank prohibiting the bank from making payment to the beneficiary varies according to the jurisdiction. In civil law jurisdictions, applications for injunctions against the bank are often denied since the applicant does not suffer any loss if the bank honours the credit, despite discrepant documents or obvious fraud. In such cases the bank is under no obligation to honour the credit. If it nevertheless honours the credit, the applicant is not obligated to reimburse the bank; therefore any payment made by the bank without it being obligated to do so is neutral for the applicant[63].

---

[61] Sarna, *Letters of Credit*, 3rd edition 1992, p. 8–6.
[62] As it is the case in Switzerland and Germany.
[63] Shingleton/Wilmer, *Einstweiliger Rechtsschutz im internationalen Dokumentenakkreditivgeschäft*, RIW 1991, 800; Schütze, *Das Dokumentenakkreditiv im internationalen Handelsverkehr*, 5th edition 1999, n. 537.

In other jurisdictions courts are not as reluctant to hand down injunctive orders against banks, and one finds Mareva injunctions that freeze the assets of the defendant, orders for non-payment, stay of proceedings, remission of documents or execution of documents[64].

For all forms of injunctive relief the applicant needs to furnish *prima facie* evidence to the court that the beneficiary has abused the credit. The requirements for *prima facie* evidence are rather tough, and in general courts in civil law jurisdictions hold that affidavits by the applicant are not sufficient[65].

Because of the applicant's own interest in the court's decision, the courts demand that other types of obvious evidence be presented, such as documentary evidence. Courts in jurisdictions influenced by Anglo-American case law, however, do tend to accept affidavits by the applicant as *prima facie* evidence[66]. These courts also consider non-appearance in court by the beneficiary or his failure to contest to court proceedings against him as a strong indication of fraud[67].

11. Restitution of unjust enrichment

If the applicant finds fraud after the credit has been duly honoured, he is entitled to take recourse against the beneficiary. No claims can be enforced against the bank if the beneficiary received payment after the presentation of compliant documents, or if fraud in the transaction was not obvious to the bank.

A claim based on unjust enrichment may be enforced if there is a depreciation of the applicant's assets which results in an enrichment of the beneficiary, and the absence of a judicial reason for such enrichment[68].

---

[64] Sarna, *Letters of Credit*, 3rd edition 1992, p. 8–4; Astro Exito Navegacion SA .v Southland Ent. Co., supra n. 1; Emery-Waterhouse Company v. Rhode Island Hospital Trust National Bank, 757 F2d 399 (1st Cir. 1985); see also sec. 5–109 (2) UCC which expressly provides for injunctions against the bank.

[65] See German Federal Supreme Court in BGHZ 101, 92; Supreme Court of Frankfurt am Main WM 1983, 575; Canaris, *Einwendungsausschluß und Einwendungsdurchgriff bei Dokumentenakkreditiven und Außenhandelsgarantien*, Öst. Bank-Archiv 1987, 777.

[66] Western Surety Company v. Bank of Southern Oregon, abstracted at 2000 Annual Survey 393; Gerald Metals, Inc. v. UBS AG, 1999 Conn. Super. Lexis 2901, abstracted at 2000 Annual Survey 322.

[67] Establishments Esefka Int. Anstalt v. Central Bank of Nigeria [1979] Ll. Rep. 447; Harfield, *Enjoining Letter of Credit Transactions*, 95 Banking LJ 596 (1978).

[68] Sarna, *Letters of Credit*, 3rd edition 1992, p. 8–3.

A claim based on unjust enrichment against the beneficiary is not available to the applicant if the bank has made payment despite obvious fraud in the transaction. In such a case, the bank is not entitled to reimbursement by the applicant, and the applicant may demand repayment by the bank of any monies advanced to the bank for payment of the credit. Consequently, there is no loss by the applicant. If the bank has made payment despite its knowledge of the beneficiary's acting in bad faith, the bank may not subsequently seek recovery from the beneficiary, since it knowingly made the payment without having the duty to do so.

The specific requirements concerning the recovery of unjust enrichment are determined by the governing law. What constitutes the applicable law depends on the laws germane to the relationship that forms the basis of the payment resulting in the unjust enrichment. According to conflict of law principles applying to documentary credits[69], claims based on unjust enrichment by the bank against the beneficiary are governed by the laws of the country of the bank's location. If an advising bank, a nominated or a confirming bank is involved, the law governing the claim for unjust enrichment depends on whether the involvement of a second bank results in the application of the law of the second bank's place of business. The law applying to the recovery claim by the applicant against the beneficiary is the law that governs the underlying transaction.

If the parties to one of the relationships agree on a choice of law, this choice of law will also prevail for the recovery of unjust enrichments.

12. Transfer of documentary credit

12.1 Transferability

Article 48 of UCP 500 contains a comprehensive but not all-embracing provision on the transferability of documentary credits. Article 48 serves to harmonize what was previously confusing terminology. The terms, "divisible", "fractionable", "assignable" or "transmissible" are disregarded and only a designation of "transferable" is relevant (see sub-Article 48(b)).

According to Article 48, the credit may be transferred only once. If a credit is designated as transferable it may be divided into separate parts without specific authorization by the bank. The fractions of a transferable credit can be transferred separately if partial shipments/drawings are not prohibited. The aggregate of the amounts of the fractions of the credit may not exceed

---

[69] See section 6 of this book.

the amount of the original credit. The transfer of all fractions is deemed to be only one transfer, and each of the transferees is regarded as a second beneficiary.

Unless otherwise provided, the transferees of fractions of a credit may not transfer them further[70]. The credit must be designated as transferable.

It is disputed whether the bank must consent to the individual transfer in addition to opening a credit that is designated as transferable. Sub-Article 48(c) provides that the transferring bank is under no obligation to effect a transfer, except in the manner expressly consented to by the transferring bank. Some commentators regard the specific consent requirement as a superfluous and impractical accumulation of the transferring bank's rights[71]. Sub-Article 48(c) is meant to protect the bank against a transfer of the credit to an unreliable creditor, and that is the principal reason an additional consent by the bank is required[72].

In general, the credit may be transferred only with the conditions of the original credit, except for amendments concerning the amount of the credit, any unit price stated therein, the expiry date, the last date for presentation of documents and the period of shipments and the insurance cover, if applicable. These terms may be reduced or curtailed (see sub-Article 48 (h)).

For reasons of competition it may be necessary not to disclose the name of the applicant. In such cases, the name of the applicant may be substituted by the name of the first beneficiary. The invoice to be presented then must be issued in the name of the first beneficiary.

12.2 Legal nature of the transfer

The legal implications of the transfer of the credit are in dispute. Legal scholars often see the transfer of the credit as an assignment[73]. Because of

---

[70] Jack, *Documentary Credits*, 2nd edition 1993, p. 238.

[71] Gutteridge/Megrah, *The Law of Bankers' Documentary Credits*, 7th edition 1984, p. 101; Stapel, *Die einheitlichen Richtlinien und Gebräuche für Dokumenten-Akkreditive der internationalen Handelskammer in der Fassung von 1993*, 1998, p. 260.

[72] Lombardini, *Droit et pratique du crédit documentaire*, Zurich 1994, p. 182; Avancini/Iro/Koziol, *Österreichiches Bankvertragsrecht*, vol. II, 1993, n. 4/110; Bank Negara Indonesia 1946 v. Narizia (Singapore) Pte Ltd (1988) 1 W.L.R. 374 (PC) in which the court expressly stated that the bank's consent to the specific transfer of the credit is necessary.

[73] Sambo, *La techniqua de credito documentario*, 1978 p. 21; van Maele, *Transfert du crédit documentaire*, Rev. de la Banque 1954, 641; Gutteridge/Megrah, *The law of Bankers' Commercial Credits*, 7th edition 1984, p. 103; Jack, Documentary Credits, 2nd edition 1993, p. 242.

its commercial effects and the conditions stipulated by the UCP (requirement of consent by the bank, exclusion of objections resulting from the relationship between the bank and the first beneficiary), the transfer of the credit closely resembles the opening of a new credit for the benefit of the second beneficiary[74]. The prevailing view is that the transfer of a credit constitutes a new and separate undertaking of the bank to the second beneficiary[75].

According to Article 48, the transfer of the credit does not cover the assignment of proceeds from the credit. An assignment of proceeds is permitted regardless of whether the credit is designated as being transferable[76]. This is expressly clarified by Article 49 of UCP 500.

The requirements and formalities for an assignment are subject to the laws of the jurisdiction which governs it. The assignability of the claim for proceeds should be differentiated from the assignment itself. While the assignability of the claim is often determined in accordance with the laws that governed the claim itself, the assignment of the claim may be subject to another system of law, which may be agreed between the parties to the assignment.

Certain jurisdictions stipulate strict requirements or formalities for a valid assignment, such as a notification of the creditor, i.e. the bank, or formal service of such notification by a bailiff[77]. Clearly, the transfer of the credit or fractions thereof is more beneficial for the second beneficiary than a simple assignment of proceeds, since the latter depends on the enforceability of the credit and is a right having secondary importance.

13. Force majeure

As a general rule, the deadline for presentation of documents is only extended if the last day on which presentation of documents is permitted falls on a Saturday, Sunday or a bank holiday. No other reason justifies the right for a delayed presentation of

---

[74] Lombardini, *Droit et pratique du crédit documentaire*, 1994, p. 186; Gani, *La saisissabilité des droits patrimoniaux en matière d'accréditif documentaire*, 1970, p. 50; Schütze, *Das Dokumentenakkreditiv im internationalen Handelsverkehr*, 5th edition 1999, n. 343.

[75] German Federal Supreme Court WM 1996, 995; Lombardini, *Droit et pratique du crédit documentaire*, 1994, p. 186; Gani, *La saisissabilité des droits patrimoniaux en matière d'accréditif documentaire*, 1970, p. 50.

[76] Eisemann/Bontoux/Rowe, *Le crédit documentaire dans le commerce extérieur*, 1985, p. 51; Jack, *Documentary Credits*, 2nd edition, 1993, p. 247; Raith, *Das Recht des Dokumenten Akkreditivs in den USA und in Deutschland*, 1985, p. 186; Sarna, *Letters of Credit*, 3rd edition 1992, p. 7–11.

[77] This is required by French law.

documents. Article 44 of UCP 500 explicitly states that the conditions referred to in Article 17 of UCP 500 (which deals with *force majeure*) will not result in an extension of the period for presentation of the documents or the expiry date. In other words, the risk of an incident of *force majeure* affecting the banks' business is borne by the beneficiary[78].

Article 17 only discharges the bank from its undertaking if documents cannot be presented due to the interruption of the bank's business. Article 17 does not apply if the beneficiary presents compliant documents in due time but if the bank cannot honour the credit because of an interruption of its business following the documents' presentation[79]. In the leading – and sole – decision by the German Federal Supreme Court on this issue, the Court had to decide on the validity of a French beneficiary's claim against a German bank based on a documentary credit issued in 1944. After the presentation of documents, French-German payment transactions ceased and the issuing bank was subjected to government control. The issuing bank claimed to be discharged from its obligations under the credit due to Article 13 of the 1933 version of UCP (today Article 17 of UCP 500). The Court rejected the issuing bank's argument and ruled that it remained bound to its commitment if documents were presented in good time. A subsequent interruption of the bank's business was considered to be irrelevant to the application of the *force majeure* provision of the UCP, and the credit was ordered to be honoured after resumption of the bank's business, even if the credit had then expired[80].

Although Article 17 appears to contain a straightforward rule, it raises certain issues that require further consideration. The term "Act of God" is translated as *force majeure* since some jurisdictions are unfamiliar with the concept of an Act of God caused exclusively by violence of nature without any contributory human action. In such jurisdictions it is doubtful whether riots, civil commotions, insurrection, wars, strikes or lock-outs will meet the criteria of *force majeure*.

Considering that the UCP's role has been to harmonize international practices, such an interpretation should be rejected. It is not necessary that the causes referred to in Article 17 qualify as *force majeure* in every individual jurisdiction[81].

---

[78] Nielsen, *Neue Richtlinien für Dokumenten-Akkreditive*, 2nd edition 2001, n. 291.

[79] Decision by the German Federal Supreme Court of November 19, 1959, WM 1960, 38 et seq.

[80] Decision by the German Federal Supreme Court of November 19, 1959, WM 1960, 38 (40); see also Dekker, *Case Studies on Documentary Credits*, ICC Publication No. 459, 1989, p. 62; Nielsen, *Neue Richtlinien für Dokumenten-Akkreditive*, 2nd edition 2001, n. 123; Avancini/Iro/Koziol, *Österreichisches Bankvertragsrecht* vol. II, 1993, n. 4/104.

[81] Schütze, *Das Dokumentenakkreditiv im internationalen Handelsverkehr*, 5th ed. 1999, n. 451.

Such an interpretation would have the undesired effect of having the application of Article 17 differ from country to country. This is clear when looking at strikes and lock-outs whose qualification as being incidents of *force majeure* is either denied by certain jurisdictions or only regarded as *force majeure* under narrow conditions[82]. The original English wording of Article 17 does not create such doubts, since riots, wars, strikes and the like do not qualify as Acts of God, and consequently their consequences must be sufficient to meet the conditions of Article 17.

Furthermore the phrase "other causes beyond their control" raises doubts of interpretation. The general nature of these words could lead to the assumption that this is a catch-all phrase[83]. Such an assumption, however, raises the question of why the UCP names specific circumstances in Article 17 at all, since the incidents named usually constitute causes beyond the bank's control.

Because of the apparent rigidity of Article 17, there appears to be no room for a catch-all provision. The term "other causes" shows that Article 17 is not limited to explicitly named situations. However, the explicit references to named events in the Article gives these events a certain importance. Article 17, according to some commentators, should be interpreted in light of the *ejusdem generis* rule, which provides that where specific words are used followed by general terms, the latter are to have the same weight as the specific words[84].

Consequently, it can be argued that Article 17 does not cover all adverse effects beyond the control of banks, only those explicitly referred to.

It is noteworthy that only the bank whose business is interrupted is released from its commitment. If the credit is confirmed by another bank, this bank may not refuse payment by referring to the interruption of the issuing bank's business.

---

[82] French law regards strikes as *force majeure* when the strike affects a complete industry, see Paris, Dalloz, *Recueil periodique et critique mensuel* 1904, 2 (73), while Anglo-American legal systems never regard strikes as *force majeure*. Balossini, *Norme ed Usini Uniformi Relativi ai Crediti Documentari*, 4th edition 1988, p. 288, is right in assuming that the controversial treatment of labour-related calamities in the individual jurisdictions has been the reason for their separate position in Article 17. In the 1974 revision the wording of the *force majeure* clause was changed for the sole purpose of eliminating doubts as to whether strikes and lock-outs need to meet any other quality in order to trigger the application of Article 17; see Wheble, *Uniform Customs and Practice for Documentary Credits (1974 revision)*, JBusL 1975, 281 (283).

[83] Balossini, *Norme ed Usini Uniformi Relativi ai Crediti Documentari*, 4th edition 1988, p. 288; von Westphalen, *Die Einheitlichen Richtlinien und Gebräuche für Dokumentenak-kreditive (1974) und Einheitlichen Richtlinien für Inkassi im Licht des AGB-Gesetzes*, WM 1980, 178 (182).

[84] Hedley/Hedley, *Bills of Exchange and Bankers' Documentary Credits*, 4th edition 2001, p. 298; Ventris, *Banker's Documentary Credits*, First Supplement to 2nd edition 1985, p. 22; Fontane, *Höhere Gewalt im Dokumentenakkreditivgeschäft*, 2001, p. 133.

The confirmation creates a separate undertaking that remains in force regardless of whether another bank is discharged from its obligations under the credit[85].

14. Statute of limitations

The UCP do not address the statute of limitations on claims arising from a documentary credit. The expiry date of the documentary credit only stipulates the latest date for the presentation of documents. If the beneficiary presents compliant documents in due time, his claim for honouring the credit comes into effect and remains in existence until the statute of limitations applicable to that claim expires.

The statute of limitations is a function of the substantive law that applies to the payment claim. Since there is no uniform system of laws that applies to the credit as such, one needs to determine the applicable law for each payment claim under the credit[86].

According to the conflict of law principles mentioned above[87], the beneficiary's claim for honouring the credit is barred by an elapse of time that is determined by the laws of the country of the confirming or issuing bank. The issuing bank's claim for reimbursement against the applicant is subject to the laws of the bank's location, and a nominated bank's claim for reimbursement from the issuing bank is subject to the laws of the nominated bank's location.

The applicable substantive law not only determines the statute of limitations of these claims, but also the suspension or interruption of the said statute and other requirements for rendering the statute effective.

---

[85] Wessely, *Die Unabhängigkeit der Akkreditivverpflichtung von Deckungsverhältnis und Kaufvertrag*, 1974, n. 26; Bandomir, *Risikoaspekte bei Akkreditivbestätigungen*, Bank-Betrieb, 1967, 170.
[86] See section 6.1 of this book.
[87] See section 6 of this book.

Part Two
Country Statutes

Austria

General Remarks

There are no special statutory provisions in Austrian law dealing with documentary credits[1]. Nevertheless, there is rich jurisprudence and legal literature on the subject[2]. An important decision of the Austrian Supreme Court dating from 1994[3] examines the case of a fraudulent use of a credit and confirms the continuous position of Austrian jurisprudence according to which the issuing bank may – and with regard to the applicant is obligated to – refuse payment to the beneficiary in case of fraud. In the case of a chain of banks, the Austrian Supreme Court applies the principles which have been developed for the so-called direct claims (*Einwendungsdruchgriff*) in abstract bank guarantees. The beneficiary is obliged to enforce its claim under the credit prior to enforcing claims resulting from the trade transaction. Only if the beneficiary's claim under the credit is not successful may the beneficiary enforce rights resulting from the trade transaction[4].

---

[1] Regarding certain practical issues, see Katzenberger, *DCI*, vol. 1/1, p. 18; vol. 2/4, p. 21; Hertel, *DCI*, vol. 1/4, p. 16; vol. 4/2, p. 20; vol. 6/2, p. 18, in particular with regard to drafts required under documentary credits.

[2] See Avancini/Iro/Koziol, *Österreichisches Bankvertragsrecht*, vol. II, 1993, p. 657 et seq.; Schinnerer, *Rechtsfragen im internationalen Akkreditivgeschäft*, ZfRV 1961, p. 347 et seq.

[3] *OGH ÖBA* 1996, 64, commented by Avancini ÖBA 1996, p. 66 et seq. and Schefold, *IPRax* 1996, p. 347 et seq.

[4] See Katzenberger, *DCI*, vol. 3/4, p. 18, who reports on a decision of the Austrian Supreme Court dating from 1996.

Bahrain

General Remarks

Articles 317 to 326 of the Commercial Code of 1987[5] cover documentary credits. These provisions correspond to the Kuwaiti statutory provisions in respect of their wording and also their application in practice.

Commercial Code

Article 317

1. The documentary credit is an agreement by which the bank undertakes to issue a credit upon a customer's (the applicant's) request for the benefit of a third party (the beneficiary) which is guaranteed by documents that represent transported goods or goods ready for transport.

2. The documentary credit shall be independent from the contract for which it is issued. The bank shall remain alien to such contract.

Article 318

The documents against which payments, acceptance or discounting are to be made shall be specified in the request to issue the documentary credit, its confirmation or notification.

Article 319

If the documents comply with the terms and conditions of the documentary credit, the issuing bank shall effect payment, acceptance or discounting as provided for in the credit.

---

[5] Law No. 7/1987.

Article 320

1. The documentary credit may be confirmed or revocable.

2. The credit opening contract shall define expressly the type of the credit. In the absence of such express definition the credit shall be deemed revocable.

Article 321

The revocable credit does not create an obligation of the bank to the beneficiary. The bank may modify or cancel the credit at all times either at its own initiative or the applicant's request without being required to notify the beneficiary, provided, however, that the modification or cancellation is done in good faith and in a reasonable time.

Article 322

1. By an irrevocable credit the bank undertakes a direct and definite obligation to the beneficiary or any good faith holder of the documents specified in the application to issue the credit.

2. An irrevocable documentary credit may not be cancelled or modified unless all concerned parties agree.

3. An irrevocable credit may be confirmed by another bank which then undertakes a direct and definite obligation to the beneficiary.

4. The simple notification of opening a documentary credit forwarded to the beneficiary via another bank shall not be deemed a confirmation of the credit.

Article 323

1. An irrevocable documentary credit shall contain an expiry date for its validity by which the documents need to be presented to effect payment, acceptance or discounting.

2. If the expiry date of the credit's validity falls on a bank holiday the validity period shall be extended to the first working day following the bank holiday.

3. Except for bank holidays, the credit's validity shall not be extended even if the expiry date falls in a period during which the bank's business is interrupted by *force majeure*, unless the applicant expressly agrees to an extension.

Bahrain

Article 324

1. The bank shall examine whether the documents comply with the instructions of the applicant of the credit.

2. If the bank refuses the documents it shall immediately notify the beneficiary by specifying the reasons for refusal.

Article 325

1. The bank does not assume any liability if the presented documents on their face appear to comply with the applicant's instructions.

2. The bank shall neither be liable for the performance of consignors and insurers of the goods for which payment the credit has been issued, their quality, weight, condition, packaging or value.

Article 326

The documentary credit may not be assigned in part or in whole unless the issuing bank is authorized by the applicant to make payment on the credit in accordance with the applicant's instructions in part or in full to one or several third parties. The credit may not be assigned unless the concerned bank agrees to the assignment. The credit may be assigned only once unless otherwise agreed upon.

Article 327

If the applicant does not pay to the bank the value of the consignment documents according to the terms of the credit within three months running from the date of notification to the applicant that the documents have been presented, the bank may sell the goods in accordance with the execution proceedings applicable to commercially pledged property.

Bolivia

General Remarks

The Bolivian Commercial Code of 1978[6] governs documentary credits in Articles 1394 to 1408. Article 1408 provides for the application of the UCP in the Articles' prevailing version unless otherwise provided.

Commercial Code

CREDITS

Article 1394 [Concept]

A documentary credit is an agreement by which a bank directly or through a correspondent undertakes for the account and in accordance with the instructions of the applicant to pay a specified amount or to pay, accept or negotiate drafts upon presentation of documents which comply with the terms and conditions which are agreed upon in the agreement.

Article 1395 [Contents of credit document]

The credit document shall contain at least the following:
1. name of the issuing bank and the correspondent bank, if any;
2. name of the applicant (purchaser);
3. name of the beneficiary (seller);
4. maximum amount to be paid or for which drafts may be endorsed for the account of the issuing bank;
5. time during which the credit may be used;
6. specification of documents to be presented and to be taken up for using the credit;
7. place and time of issuance and the signature of the issuing bank (Articles 712a, 716 Commercial Code).

---

[6] Decreto-Ley No. 14379.

Bolivia

Article 1396 [Types of credit]

Credits may be revocable or irrevocable, confirmed or not confirmed, revolving or not revolving or transferable. The credit may have other characteristics if it is expressly provided for in the agreement (Articles 1399, 1408, 1409, Commercial Code).

Article 1397 [Revocability]

The revocable credit is not a definite undertaking by the bank to the beneficiary. It may be amended or cancelled during its validity period upon request without notification to the beneficiary.

In the absence of a specific stipulation the credit shall be deemed revocable even if the credit bears an expiry date.

Article 1398 [Irrevocability]

If a credit provides for irrevocability the issuing bank undertakes the definite obligation for the benefit of the beneficiary provided that the terms and conditions of the credit are met. Each subsequent modification or cancellation requires all interested parties' consent.

A credit which is not used by the beneficiary during its validity period may be revoked by the issuing bank at any time even if it is denominated as irrevocable. If the credit is used in part, the credit's characteristics sustain with respect to the remaining part.

Article 1399 [Notification and confirmation of the credit]

An irrevocable credit may be notified to the beneficiary by another bank or a correspondent without any obligation of the latter by mere notification. If the issuing bank, however, authorizes the other bank or the correspondent to confirm the irrevocable credit and such bank does so, the confirmation creates a joint and several and definite liability.

Article 1400 [Undertaking of the issuing bank]

By the credit opening agreement the issuing bank undertakes the following principal obligations (Articles 1428, 1346a, 1386 Commercial Code):

1. To register the credit in its records for the benefit of the beneficiary and to release the credit document to the beneficiary either directly or through a correspondent and to notify the beneficiary of the issuance and the terms and conditions of the credit.

2. To take up complying documents received directly or through a correspondent, to examine them with diligence, to notify the applicant thereof or forward the documents to the applicant (Articles 535, 678, 1449, Commercial Code).

3. To pay the credit's amount or to accept or discount drafts drawn by the beneficiary. The issuing bank may use a correspondent which in the name of the applicant makes payment, accepts or discounts drafts depending on the type of credit (Articles 1400, 745, 1723, Commercial Code).

Article 1401 [Obligations of the applicant]

The applicant undertakes the following principal obligations:

1. To accept the documents, which evidence that the goods have been loaded on board, promptly after notification by the issuing bank or at the latest within the subsequent three days;

2. To reimburse the bank for the amount paid during the periods as set forth in the agreement which the bank has paid for the benefit of the beneficiary unless the applicant deposits such amount prior to payment, provided that the payment is made in compliance with the instructions given to the bank (Articles 1400, 1428, Commercial Code);

3. To pay the expenses, interest and commission for the issuance of the credit regardless of whether the credit has been used or not except in the case that the bank has unliterary revoked the credit; and

4. Upon request of the bank to provide personal or real collateral to secure the transaction.

Article 1402 [Other types of credit]

If not expressly agreed upon payment in cash, the agreement between the applicant and the bank may provide for a *credito di firma* acceptance, guaranteed credit or *credito di fianza o guarantia*, subject to the provisions of this law (Article 1396, Commercial Code).

Boliva

Article 1403 [Exceptions]

The issuing bank may only raise the objections against the beneficiary provided for in the credit document or personal objections.

Article 1404 [Transfer]

The credit is transferable if the credit document expressly provides so. If the credit is transferred in partial amounts their sum may add up to its total amount unless such partial transfer is expressly prohibited. The credit only may be used in parts if so permitted.

Article 1405 [Liability of the bank to the applicant]

The issuing bank is liable to the applicant according to the provisions of professional mandates and shall ensure that the documents presented by the beneficiary precisely comply with the contents of the credit document.

Article 1406 [Expiry]

If the credit does not provide for an expiry date the credit shall be valid for six months running from the date of notification to the beneficiary.

Article 1407 [Credit and underlying transactions]

Due to its nature the credit is separate from the purchase agreement and any other transaction to which the issued credit relates. Due to this nature neither the issuing bank nor the correspondence bank, if any, assumes any responsibility for the form, quality, authenticity, or legal effect of any of the documents related to the credit transaction. The bank is neither liable with regard to the conditions, quantity, weight, quality, condition of packaging, shipment or value of the goods that are referred to in the documents, nor with regard to the general or specific terms provided for in the documents, good faith actions, the actions of the consignor, the shipper or any other person. The bank does not assume any liability for the liquidity and reputation of the person responsible for the shipment or the goods' insurers (Article 1451 Commercial Code).

Article 1408 [Additional application of the Uniform Customs and Practices for Documentary Credits]

Any issue not covered by this paragraph shall be governed by the Uniform Customs and Practices for Documentary Credits in their prevailing version.

Bulgaria

General Remarks

The Bulgarian law on documentary credits is governed by Articles 435 – 441 of part III of the Commercial Code[7]. The Bulgarian statutory provisions do not deviate from the UCP 500.

Commercial Code

CREDIT – DEFINITION AND FORM

Article 435

1. The credit is a unilateral written declaration by a bank, by which it undertakes to pay the credit amount to the person referred to in the credit if such person presents to the bank the document described in the credit within a period stipulated in the credit and meets all other conditions of the credit. The credit becomes effective upon notification to such person.

2. The bank may instruct another bank to receive the documents, to examine them together with all other conditions of the credit, and pay the amount.

3. The documents shall be examined by an outsider.

4. For payment of the credit's amount only such conditions shall be relevant which are named in the credit.

5. Upon expiration of the period the credit becomes ineffective.

IRREVOCABILITY OF THE CREDIT

Article 436

Unless otherwise provided for by the credit the credit shall be deemed irrevocable and may only be revoked and amended upon the third party's approval.

---

[7] Effective since 1 November 1976.

REVOCABLE CREDIT

Article 437

The revocable credit may be revoked unilaterally by the bank as long it is not executed.

FRACTIONABILITY AND NON-ASSIGNABILITY OF THE CREDIT

Article 438

Unless otherwise agreed the credit is fractionable and not assignable.

CONFIRMED CREDIT

Article 439

If an irrevocable credit is confirmed by another bank, such bank undertakes to pay the credit's amount directly and independently.

MANDATE AGREEMENT AND CREDIT

Article 440

The provisions on mandate agreements shall apply to the relationship between the applicant and the issuing bank and the relationships between the banks under the credit.

REMUNERATION

Article 441

The applicant shall pay a remuneration to the bank.

Canada

The Canadian statutes do not contain any specific provisions on documentary credits. Canadian jurisprudence acknowledges internationally established customs and practices for documentary credit transactions. Autonomy of the credit transaction is regarded as a cardinal principle[8].

The principle of autonomy does not imply that a court is prevented from considering any and all aspects of the underlying transaction. Unequivocal language of the credit document may be interpreted by taking into account the wording of the ancillary documents[9]. In addition, fraud by the beneficiary limits the beneficiary's rights under the credit[10].

Canadian courts recognize a choice of law by the parties. In the absence of a choice of law they take the view that the applicable law is the one to which the credit transaction has the "closest and most real connection"[11]. In this respect the principle of autonomy results in the application of different systems of law for the credit transaction and the trade transaction. A documentary credit is considered to have the closest relation to the location of the issuing bank. If a correspondent bank is involved, it is considered to have the closest relation to such correspondent bank's location[12].

---

[8] Bank of Montreal v. Mitchell (1997) 143 D.L.R. (4th) 697; Finch, *DCI*, vol. 4/3 p. 16 and *DCI*, vol. 5/2 p. 19.
[9] Sarna, *Letters of Credit*, 3rd ed., Ontario 1992, p. 5-2.
[10] Sarna, *Letters of Credit*, 3rd ed., Ontario 1992, p. 5-8.
[11] Sarna, *Letters of Credit*, 3rd ed., Ontario 1992, p. 9-4.
[12] Sarna, *Letters of Credit*, 3rd ed., Ontario 1992, p. 9-5; for further issues see Than Htut, *DCI*, vol. 1/3 p. 15; *DCI*, vol. 2/3 p. 17; *DCI*, vol. 3/3 p. 20; Finch, *DCI*, vol. 4/3 p. 16; *DCI*, vol. 5/2 p. 19; Kwok, *DCI*, vol. 6/1 p. 15; see also Kwok, *DCI*, vol. 4/1 p. 19, reporting on an uncertainty in Canadian law regarding the interpretation of Article 23 (a) (i) UCP 500.

Canada

Colombia

General Remarks

Articles 1408 – 1415 of the new Commercial Code[13] contain provisions on documentary credits. These provisions codify internationally acknowledged principles, such as the express autonomy of the credit from the trade transaction in Article 1415[14].

Commercial Code

Article 1404

A documentary credit is an agreement by which the bank undertakes to pay an amount either directly or through a correspondent up to a maximum amount, or to pay, accept or negotiate drafts drawn by the beneficiary upon instructions, and request by a customer and upon presentation specified documents if they are in conformity with the agreed terms and conditions.

Article 1409

The credit must contain:
1. name of the issuing bank and the correspondent, if any;
2. name of the holder of the credit document or the applicant;
3. name of the beneficiary;
4. maximum amount to be paid or for which drafts may be drawn for the account of the bank issuing drafts or the bank issuing the credit;
5. period during which the credit may be used; and
6. documents and requisites to be presented or satisfied for using of the credit.

Article 1410

The documentary credit may be revocable or irrevocable. The credit shall be revocable unless otherwise expressly provided for in the credit.

---

[13] Nuevo codico de comercio, Decreto-Ley 410/1971.
[14] For issues arising in practice, see Medina Riog, *DCI*, vol. 1/4 p. 16.

Article 1411

The issuing bank may revoke the credit at any time as long it is not used by the beneficiary. If the credit is used in part its characteristics shall be sustained with regard to the remaining parts.

Article 1412

An irrevocable credit shall provide for the time during which it may be used. In the absence of such provision the revocable credit may be used during a maximum period of six months running from the date of notification to the beneficiary by the bank at which the credit may be used.

Article 1413

The credit is assignable if expressly provided for. Unless expressly prohibited, the credit may be assigned in parts up to its maximum amount. The credit may be used in parts only if is expressly permitted by the credit.

Article 1414

The notification of the credit by another bank as intermediary bank does not impose any obligation on such bank unless such bank undertakes to confirm the credit. In such case the confirming bank undertakes an obligation to the beneficiary at the same terms and conditions as the issuing bank from the day of the confirmation.

Article 1415

The credit is independent from the agreement to which the issued credit applies. Thus, neither the issuing nor the correspondent bank, if any, undertakes any liability with regard to the form, quantity, authenticity, falsification or legal effects of any of the documents relating to the relevant agreement; the issuing bank undertakes no responsibility for the type, quantity, weight, quality, conditions, packaging, shipment or value of the goods which are represented by the documents; the banks undertake no responsibility with regard to the general or specific conditions which are referred to by the documents, with regard to good faith or with regard to actions of the consignor or the shipper or any other person; they are neither liable with regard to the liquidity, reputation, etc. of the persons who are entrusted with the shipment of the goods or the insurers of the goods.

Colombia

Czech Republic

General Remarks

The law of documentary credits[15] is governed by §§ 682 – 691 of the Czech Commercial Code[16]. The provisions are not as comprehensive as the UCP 500. The issues addressed by Czech provisions do not deviate from the UCP 500.

Commercial Code

20TH CHAPTER – AGREEMENT ON THE ISSUANCE OF A CREDIT

§ 682 [Basic provisions]

1. By the agreement on the issuance of a credit the bank becomes liable to the applicant to make a specified payment to a third party (beneficiary) according to the applicant's instructions and for his account if the beneficiary meets the set forth conditions by a specified time; the applicant undertakes to pay a fee to the bank.

2. The agreement is required to be in writing.

§ 683 [Issuance of the credit]

1. The bank notifies the beneficiary in compliance with the agreement that a credit has been issued for his benefit and informs the beneficiary on the credit's terms. The credit document shall include the payment which the bank undertakes to make, the term of the credit and the credit's conditions which the beneficiary has to meet within such term so that beneficiary may demand payment from the bank.

2. After execution of the agreement the bank shall make the notification according to subsection 1 without undue delay unless the agreement indicates that the notification shall only be made upon instruction by the applicant.

---

[15] As to the prevailing practice, see Andrle, *DCI*, vol. 6/1, p. 16.
[16] Law No. 513/1991.

Czech Republic

3. The bank's liability to the beneficiary becomes existent by the notification according to subsection 1.

4. The liability of the applicant to the bank becomes existent upon issuance of the credit.

5. The credit document may provide in particular for the bank's liability to pay a specified amount or to accept a draft.

§ 684 [Amount of the fee]

If no fee for the issuance of the credit has been agreed upon the applicant shall pay the fee that is customary at the time of the execution of the agreement.

LEGAL STATUS OF THE BANK TO THE BENEFICIARY

§ 685 [Undertaking by the bank]

The undertaking of the letter of credit by the bank is independent from the relationship between the applicant and the beneficiary.

§ 686 [Revocable and irrevocable credits]

1. If the credit document does not provide for the revocability of the credit the bank may only amend or revoke the credit upon approval of the applicant and the beneficiary.

2. If the credit document provides for revocability the bank may amend or revoke the credit with effect for the beneficiary as long as the conditions of the credit are not met.

3. The amendment or revocation of a credit may only be made in writing.

§ 687 [Additional banks]

1. If an irrevocable credit was confirmed by another bank upon the issuing bank's instruction the beneficiary's claim to performance against such bank arises at the time such bank confirms the credit to the beneficiary. The issuing bank and the bank which confirms the credit are jointly and severally liable to the beneficiary.

2. A letter of credit confirmed by a second bank may only be amended or revoked upon such bank's approval.

Czech Republic

3. If the bank which confirms the credit honours the credit in compliance with the credit's terms such bank has a claim to performance against the issuing bank.

§ 688 [Liability for incorrect notification]

If the issuance of the credit is accomplished through another bank such bank is liable for the damage that results from the incorrectness of the notification. However, such bank is not liable for the credit itself.

DOCUMENTARY CREDIT

§ 689 [Commitment by the bank]

If all documents referred to in the documentary credit are presented to the bank during the credit's lifetime the bank is obligated to the beneficiary to perform under the credit.

§ 690 [Strict compliance]

1. The bank undertakes to examine the compliance of the presented documents with the conditions set forth by the credit with adequate diligence.

2. The bank shall be liable to the applicant for the loss or destruction of the documents taken over by the beneficiary unless the damage could not have been avoided if adequate diligence was applied.

§ 691

The provisions of §§ 689 to 690 apply *mutadis mutandis* to credits which provide for a claim to performance under conditions other than the presentation of the documents.

Egypt

General Remarks

The new Egyptian Commercial Code[17] covers documentary credits in Articles 341 to 350. Article 341 subsection 3 of the new Code includes a fall-back clause for the application of the Uniform Customs and Practice of ICC. The UCP are to be applied as subordinated provisions. However, the Code does not indicate which revision of the UCP shall be applied. It appears that the prevailing revision of the UCP shall be applicable.

The Code does not include provisions regarding conflicts of law. The Egyptian Court of Appeals subjects documentary credits to the laws of the place of performance. In the case of an issuing bank in London and an advising bank domiciled in Egypt, the court regarded such place of performance to be in Egypt[18].

Commercial Code

Article 341

1. The documentary credit is a contract by which the bank undertakes to open a credit in favour of a third party (the "beneficiary") upon its customer's (the "applicant") request, supported by documents that represent transported goods or goods ready for transport.

2. The documentary credit is separate from the contract for which it is issued. The bank shall not become party to that contract.

3. The Uniform Customs and Practice for Documentary Credits by the International Chamber of Commerce shall apply unless the articles of this section contain special provisions.

---

[17] Law No. 17/1999.
[18] Decision of February 27, 1984 re: Nil Exports v. Midland Bank; see Jung, *Ägyptisches Internationales Vertragsrecht*, 1999, p. 66, including case study.

Egypt

Article 342

The issuing bank shall honour the credit by payment, bank acceptance or negotiation, as agreed upon in the credit, if the documents comply with the conditions set forth in the credit.

Article 343

1. The documentary credit may be revocable or irrevocable.

2. If the revocabilityis not explicitly agreed on the credit shall be irrevocable.

Article 344

A revocable credit shall not create any obligation by the bank to the beneficiary. A revocable credit may be modified or cancelled at the bank's discretion or upon the applicant's request without prior notice to the beneficiary unless the credit has been fulfilled.

Article 345

1. The bank's obligations under an irrevocable documentary credit shall be absolute and direct to the beneficiary and to any *bona fide* holder of a debenture that was withdrawn in fulfilment of the contract for which the credit was issued.

2. The irrevocable documentary credit may not be revoked or modified unless all concerned parties consent.

Article 346

1. The irrevocable documentary credit may be confirmed by another bank which thereby is definitively and directly committed to the beneficiary.

2. The simple notification of an irrevocable documentary credit which is forwarded to the beneficiary through another bank shall not be considered a confirmation of the credit by this bank.

Article 347

1. The bank shall ascertain the compliance of the documents with the applicant's instructions for opening the credit.

2. If the bank refuses the documents it shall promptly inform the applicant and indicate the reasons therefor.

Article 348

1. No liability of the bank shall be incurred if the documents appear to be in compliance with the instructions by the applicant.

2. The bank shall not have any liability for the goods that are paid by the credit.

Article 349

The documentary credit shall not be transferred or divided unless the issuing bank is permitted to transfer the whole or part of it to a third party other than the first beneficiary upon instructions by the beneficiary. The transfer shall not be effective unless the bank approves it. The credit may be transferred only once unless otherwise agreed.

Article 350

If the applicant does not reimburse the bank for the value of the documents conforming to the credit's conditions within six months from the date of notification that the documents were received, the bank may execute the goods according to the procedures of execution of commercially pledged objects.

Egypt

El Salvador

General Remarks

Documentary Credits are governed by Articles 1125 to 1137 of the Commercial Code.

Commercial Code

Article 1125

By an agreement on the issuance of a credit the issuing entity undertakes to the applicant to pay a specified amount to a third party upon presentation of documents which serve as a guarantee and the first party undertakes to pay a remuneration of the costs incurred by the consummation of the transaction.

Instead of a cash payment to the third party the issuing entity may undertake to issue drafts for the benefit of the third party.

Article 1126

The issuing entity may only raise objections against the beneficiary which result from the agreement and personal objections.

Article 1127

A credit which is not denominated revocable and for which a validity period has been agreed upon shall be deemed irrevocable.

Article 1128

The revocable credit may be cancelled at any time by the issuing entity. However, such entity is obliged to inform the applicant and the beneficiary of its decision.

Article 1129

An irrevocable credit binds the issuing bank to the beneficiary and may not be modified or cancelled without all interested parties' consent.

Article 1130

The irrevocable credit may be notified to the beneficiary by appointment of another commercial entity which shall be severally and jointly liable for the satisfaction of the credit if such entity confirms the credit.

Article 1131

A credit which does not contain an expiry date is deemed to be valid for a period of six months running from the date of its notification to the beneficiary.

Article 1132

The issuance of a documentary credit which is not notified as provided for in Article 1130 shall be effected by a credit document which contains the conditions, requirements and the nature of the issued credit.

Article 1133

The issuing bank shall examine the documents as indicated by the applicant. In the absence of such indication it shall examine the following documents:

I. for sea or airway transport: bill of lading in negotiable form

II. for land transport: shipping bill in negotiable form

III. for international transactions: consular documents

IV. in all cases: a policy or confirmation of transferable insurance and an invoice for the goods.

The issuing bank is not required to request such documents if the beneficiary provides – in the bank's judgment – sufficient evidence that the insurance cover has been established by the applicant or by the recipient of the goods.

Article 1134

The issuing bank shall be liable for the formal regularity and compliance of the documents with the terms of the credit opening agreement.

Article 1135

The issuing bank shall not be liable:

I. for the contents or the authenticity of the presented documents

II. for the condition, quality, quantity and price of the goods referred to in the documents

El Salvador

El Salvador

III. for the accuracy of the translation of the relevant agreement

IV. for the loss of documents during transport; delay, defects or transmission errors of telegraphic correspondence

V. for non-compliance of its instructions by the parties which were appointed by the applicant unless the issuing bank appointed such third parties at its own initiative.

Article 1136

Unless otherwise agreed, the documentary credit is not assignable. If the documentary credit is assignable the terms and conditions of the original shall be respected except for the credit's amount, which may be reduced, and except for its validity period, which may be shortened.

If the assignment incurs costs such costs shall be borne by the initial beneficiary unless otherwise agreed.

Article 1137

The authority to assign the credit also includes transferring it to another place. The cost of such transaction shall be borne by the initial beneficiary unless other modifications are made.

Germany

General Remarks

The laws of the former German Democratic Republic contained specific provisions dealing with documentary credits. §§ 256 – 258 of the Law on International Commercial Relations provided for partial – quite incomplete – coverage of the issue[19]. According to the statutory provisions of the GDR, documentary credits in principle were revocable unless expressly stipulated as irrevocable. The Law on International Commercial Relations was abolished in the course of the synchronization of German laws after the German unification. Today there are no specific statutory provisions dealing with documentary credits.

Despite the absence of statutory provisions, documentary credits are subject to intense attention in legal literature[20] and jurisprudence.

In recent times the courts have focused in particular on the interpretation of documentary credits. Considering the principles of segregation between the credit and the trade transaction and the rule of strict compliance, German courts are of the opinion that documentary credits can be subject to interpretation[21].

---

[19] Eisemann/Schütze, *Das Dokumentenakkreditiv im internationalen Handelsverkehr*, 3rd ed., 1989, p. 29 et seq., including a reprint of the provisions of the GDR; Schütze, *Zum internationalen Bankrecht der DDR*, WM 1976, p. 970 et seq.

[20] Exerpt from the abundant literature: Nielsen, *Grundlagen des Akkreditivgeschäfts – Revision 1983, 1985*; Nielsen, *Neue Richtlinien für Dokumentenakkreditive*, 1994; Nielsen, *Grundlagen des Akkreditivgeschäfts in* Schimansky/Bunte/Lwowski, *Bankrechtshandbuch*, vol. II, 1997, p. 3412 et seq.; Schütze, *Das Dokumentenakkreditiv im internationalen Handelsverkehr*, 5th ed. 1999 with a comprehensive bibliography of the available literature on p. 361 et seq.

[21] Federal Supreme Court WM 1994, 1063 commented by Schütze WuB I H2-2.94; State Supreme Court Frankfurt/Main DZWir 1997 commented by Berger; further Schütze/Fontane, *DCI*, vol. 4/4, p. 21.

Greece

General Remarks

The Greek provisions on documentary credits are the only statutory provisions on documentary credits in the European Union. Since Greek banks collectively adhere to the UCP the statutory provisions have become rather meaningless. Nevertheless, Greece intends to revise its laws on documentary credits.

The Greek provisions on documentary credits are included in the Regulation of 17 July/13 August 1923 on "Special Provisions for Stock Corporations". Articles 25 to 34 of this Regulation govern documentary credits. The statutory provisions do not show any particularities for the relationship between the beneficiary and the issuing bank. Even the involvement of correspondent banks does not have any specific impact on this relationship. Greek law, however, strengthens the position of the issuing bank toward the applicant. Article 29 provides for a pledge for the benefit of the bank on transferred securities and cash funds. This pledge comes into existence without meeting the general legal requirements for the creation of a pledge. Article 31 et seq. provide for comprehensive rights of the bank to utilize the goods.

Provisions on Documentary Credits

Article 25

1. A Documentary credit is an agreement between a banking corporation (creditor) and another party (debtor) to issue a credit for the benefit of a third party (beneficiary). By this agreement the bank undertakes to pay to such third party the credit amount upon presentation of the bill of lading. Such amount shall be reimbursed by the debtor upon forwarding the bill of lading.

2. By payment of the amount the bank acquires a pledge over the goods referred to in the bill of lading.

3. The agreement on the credit shall be in writing.

4. The agreement on the credit is a commercial transaction for both parties.

Article 26

1. The bill of lading or the waybill shall be issued or endorsed in the name of or by order of the bank or shall be presented to the bank if it is a bearer bill of lading.

2. If the parties agree in the contract on a credit that the third party shall present a full set of documents, the bank shall be obliged to demand presentation of the insurance policies and the commercial invoices in addition to the bill of lading.

3. Instead of the bill of lading the parties may agree that the third party present warehouse warrants.

Article 27

Payment to the third party can be made either by the issuing bank or by its domestic or foreign correspondent bank.

Article 28

In the absence of an agreement to the contrary

a. The bank may not revoke the credit if the third party has been advised by the bank on the issuance of the credit and the third party informed the bank that it accepted the credit, unless the bank indicated in its notification that the credit is revocable.

b. The credit shall be regarded as expired if the bank included a deadline in its notification by which the third party must present the bill of lading and the documents, and such deadline has been expired ineffectually.

Article 29

1. If the applicant hands over to the issuing bank moneys or securities as collateral for the issuance of the credit the bank shall acquire a pledge at the time of accepting such moneys or securities even if the formalities for creating a pledge are not complied with.

2. The provisions on the sale of pledged property shall apply to the forced sale of the handed-over securities.

Article 30

1. The bank shall not be liable
   a. for accidental loss of the goods
   b. for failure of any telegraph service in the transmission of telegraphs.

2. The bank shall be liable for intentional or negligent acts including negligence in the choice of the correspondent bank.

Article 31

1. The bank is authorized to sell the goods according to the provisions on the sale of pledged property if after receipt of the bills of lading at the final destination the applicant does not meet its obligation to pay its debts and to take over the goods despite request to do so.

2. Such sale may only be carried out after expiry of a period of 24 hours for perishable goods or a period of 10 days for all other goods. The period shall run from the time of the request. The type of goods shall be determined by the presiding judge of the District Court[22] based on an opinion by the President of the Chamber of Commerce if there is a Chamber of Commerce at the place of the District Court. Such opinion shall be completed within 24 hours after the time of the request.

3. If the bank carries out the sale upon permission by the presiding judge the bank shall not be liable to the debtor or a third party unless the bank acts intentionally or with gross negligence in the sale.

Article 32

If the proceeds from the sale are not sufficient to cover the bank's claims the applicant shall be liable for the remaining amount.

Article 33

If the goods have not reached their final destination prior to the agreed expiry date, the bank is authorized upon permission by the presiding judge of the court at the place of the goods' final destination.

Article 34

The provisions of this chapter shall be applied *mutadis mutandis* to the agreement on the credit by which the bank pays to the applicant a sum of money upon presentation of the bill of lading and such sum is to be reimbursed to the bank by a third party upon submission of the bill of lading.

---

[22] The original wording of the law does not include the words "judge of the District Court" and refers only to "the chairman". The subsequent wording of the provision, however, reveals the actual meaning of the term "chairman".

Guatemala

General Remarks

The Guatemalan Commercial Code of 1970[23] governs the law on documentary credits in Articles 758-765. As a result of the implementation of Article 38 UCP 1962 within §765 – as in corresponding provisions of other Latin American countries – the Commercial Code provides that credits have a term of six months unless otherwise provided for.

Commercial Code

ON THE DOCUMENTARY CREDIT

Article 758 [Documentary credit]

By the agreement on the issuing of a documentary credit the issuing bank undertakes to the applicant to assume an obligation for the benefit of a third party for the applicant's account in accordance with the terms set forth by the applicant.

Article 759 [Irrevocability]

If the credit provides for its irrevocability the credit may neither be modified nor cancelled without all involved parties' consent.

Article 760 [Joint and several liability]

The bank which notifies the issuance of the credit to the beneficiary will not be obliged by the mere notification. If such bank confirms a credit such bank shall be jointly and severally liable.

Article 761 [Objections]

The bank may only raise such objections against the beneficiary which result from the documentary credit or personal objections.

---

[23] Decreto 2-70.

Article 762 [Transferability]

The beneficiary may only transfer the credit if such right was conferred upon him by the credit.

Article 763 [Liability of the banks]

The banks are liable to the applicant according to the provisions on professional mandates and shall examine with diligence that the documents which are presented by the beneficiary conform to the regulations imposed by commercial customs.

Article 764 [Credit]

If a credit is issued to guarantee to the seller the payment of the purchase price, the issuing bank or its correspondent must not make payment prior to ensuring that the presented documents referring to the goods correspond on their face to the required form.

In such case the credit by its nature is a transaction which is independent from the sales agreement.

Article 765 [Expiration]

If the credit does not contain an expiry date, the credit shall be in force for six months running from the date of the notification of the beneficiary.

Honduras

Commercial Code

Article 898

By the agreement on the issuance of a credit the issuing bank undertakes to the applicant to make payment upon presentation of specific documents or to accept drafts which any third party may hold to secure the reimbursement of its expenses, costs and agreed remuneration.

Article 899

The issuance of a documentary credit does not cause any amendment to the existing relationship between the applicant and the beneficiary.

The issuing bank may only raise such personal objections against the beneficiary which the bank is entitled to and which result from the credit opening agreement.

Article 900

The issuance of the documentary credit may be revocable, irrevocable and confirmed. A credit which is not expressly denominated revocable and for which an expiry date has been agreed upon shall be regarded irrevocable.

Article 901

The revocable credit may be modified or cancelled without the issuing bank being required to notify the applicant thereof.

Article 902

The irrevocable credit binds the issuing bank to the beneficiary and may not be modified or cancelled in any case without all involved parties' consent.

Article 903

The irrevocable credit may be notified to the beneficiary by appointing a third party which is liable for the satisfaction of the credit if it confirms the credit.

Article 904

A credit which does not contain an expiry date shall be deemed valid for six months running from the date of its notification to the beneficiary.

Article 905

The issuance of the credit may be notified to the beneficiary by forwarding the credit document which shall contain the conditions, requirements and the type of the issued credit.

Article 906

The issuing bank shall request the documents as indicated by the applicant or in the absence of such indication the following documents:

a. in case of sea transport, a complete set of lading documents;

b. in case of transport, an air cargo negotiable waybill;

c. in any event, insurance policy or a certificate of transferable insurance and invoices for the goods; and

d. in case of international transactions, consular documents.

The issuing bank may waive its right to demand insurance documents if it receives from the beneficiary – in the opinion of the bank – sufficient evidence that the insurance is covered by the applicant or the recipient of the goods.

Article 907

The banks shall be responsible for the formal regularity and compliance of the documents with the terms of the issuance of the credit which was required by the applicant.

Article 908

Banks do not assume any liability:

a. with regard to the holder and the authenticity of the documents which are presented to the banks;

b. with regard to the conditions, the quality, the quantity or the price of the goods referred to in the documents;

c. with regard to the precision of the translation of the credit's terms and conditions;

d. in case of a loss of the documents during transport, in case of delay, expiry, errors or defaults in the transmission of wire transfers or telegrams; and

e. in case of non-compliance with further instruction by the banks whose services were used unless the bank elected the correspondent bank at its own initiative.

Article 909

Unless otherwise agreed, the credit shall be assignable. However, the terms and conditions of the original credit shall be sustained except for the amount of the credit, which may be reduced, and the validity date, which may be shortened. If the assignment incurs expenses such expenses shall be borne by the first beneficiary unless otherwise agreed.

The authority to transfer the credit includes the right to transfer it to another place. The bank's expenses which are incurred by such transactions shall be borne by the first beneficiary unless there is an agreement to the contrary. During the validity of the original credit, payment may be examined at the place to which it has been transferred.

Article 910

National and international customs shall apply to every issue that has not been covered by the parties' agreement or by the foregoing provisions.

Honduras

Hungary

Hungary

General Remarks

§14 of Decree No. 6/97 on money traffic by the President of the Hungarian Federal Reserve Bank governs the handling of credit transactions. Other than this decree there are no specific provisions on documentary credits in Hungarian law. §14 subsection 5 of the Decree explicitly refers to the UCP, to which all issued credits shall be subjected.

Decree No. 6/97

§14

1. By the documentary credit the credit institution (issuing credit institution) undertakes – on the basis of a mandate by the debtor of the underlying transaction – an obligation in its own name to pay the amount stipulated in the documentary credit to the beneficiary if compliant documents are presented and such documents are presented by the beneficiary in the stipulated period.

2. The beneficiary shall present the documents stipulated in the documentary credit – together with a demand letter – directly or via his firm's credit institution to the issuing credit institution.

3. The issuing credit institution pays to the beneficiary the amount of the documentary credit by remittance to his cash bank account referred to in the documentary credit or in the demand letter.

4. The debtor of the underlying transaction pays or reimburses the issuing credit institution the amount paid by the issuing credit institution to the beneficiary according to the provisions of the mandate.

5. The provisions of the Uniform Customs and Practice for Documentary Credits issued by the International Chamber of Commerce, Paris shall be binding for documentary credits.

6. The credit institution shall set forth in its internal rules the maximum amount on which it accepts mandates to issue documentary credits.

7. It is not possible to issue documentary credits for the benefit or at the expense of a private bank account.

Iraq

General Remarks

The Iraqi law on documentary credits is governed by Articles 273 to 282 of the Commercial Code of 1984[24]. Like some other Arab countries, Iraq has incorporated the Kuwaiti laws on documentary credits into its national laws.

Commercial Code

Article 273

1. The documentary credit is an agreement by which the bank undertakes to issue a credit upon a customer's (the applicant's) request for the benefit of a third party (the beneficiary) which is guaranteed by documents that represent transported goods or goods ready for transport.

2. The documentary credit shall be independent from the contract for which it is issued. The bank shall remain alien to such contract.

Article 274

The documents against which payments, acceptance or discounting are to be made shall be specified in the request to issue the documentary credit, its confirmation or notification.

Article 275

If the documents comply with the terms and conditions of the documentary credit, the issuing bank shall effect payment, acceptance or discounting, as provided for in the credit.

Article 276

1. The documentary credit may be confirmed or revocable.

---

[24] Law No. 30/1984

Iraq

2. The credit opening contract shall define expressly the type of the credit. In the absence of such express definition the credit shall be deemed revocable.

Article 277

The revocable credit does not create an obligation of the bank to the beneficiary. The bank may modify or cancel the credit at all times either at its own initiative or the applicant's request without being required to notify the beneficiary, provided that the modification or cancellation is done in good faith and in a reasonable time.

Article 278

1. By an irrevocable credit the bank undertakes a direct and definite obligation to the beneficiary or any good-faith holder of the documents specified in the application to issue the credit.

2. An irrevocable documentary credit may not be cancelled or modified unless all concerned parties agree.

3. An irrevocable credit may be confirmed by another bank which then undertakes a direct and definite obligation to the beneficiary.

4. The simple notification of opening a documentary credit forwarded to the beneficiary via another bank shall not be deemed a confirmation of the credit.

Article 279

1. An irrevocable documentary credit shall contain an expiry date for its validity by which the documents need to be presented to effect payment, acceptance or discounting.

2. If the expiry date of the credit's validity falls on a bank holiday the validity period shall be extended to the first working day following the bank holiday.

3. Except for bank holidays, the credit's validity shall not be extended even if the expiry date falls in a period during which the bank's business is interrupted by *force majeure*, unless the applicant expressly agrees to an extension.

Article 280

1. The bank shall examine whether the documents comply with the instructions of the applicant of the credit.

2. If the bank refuses the documents it shall immediately notify the beneficiary by specifying the reasons for refusal.

Article 281

1. The bank does not assume any liability if the presented documents on their face appear to comply with the applicant's instructions.

2. The bank shall not be liable for the performance of consignors and insurers of the goods for which payment the credit has been issued, their quality, weight, condition, packaging or value.

Article 282

The documentary credit may not be assigned in part or in whole unless the issuing bank is authorized by the applicant to make payment on the credit in accordance with the applicant's instructions in part or in full to one or several third parties. The credit may not be assigned unless the concerned bank agrees to the assignment. The credit may be assigned only once unless otherwise agreed upon.

Article 283

If the applicant does not pay to the bank the value of the consignment documents according to the terms of the credit within three months running from the date of notification to the applicant that the documents have been presented, the bank may sell the goods in accordance with the execution proceedings applicable to commercially pledged property.

Iraq

Israel

General Remarks

Israeli law does not provide for any specific statutory provisions applicable to documentary credits. On various occasions documentary credits have been the subject of court decisions[25]. Israeli courts generally recognize the principle of strict compliance and the principle of independence[26] and tend to apply principles established by Anglo-American courts.

Within narrow limits, such as in case of fraud, Israeli jurisprudence permits injunctions against the issuing bank to block the payment of a letter of credit.

A recent court decision[27] states that the issuing bank is not released from its duty to diligently examine the documents although its foreign correspondent bank found them to be compliant with the credit. The failure to examine the documents by the Israeli issuing bank was considered to constitute negligence under general contract law and the bank's claim against the applicant for reimbursement was rejected by the court.

---

[25] See Schoenfield, *DCI* vol. 2/2 p. 15; Cohen, *DCI*, vol. 3/3 p. 21; Shpayer, *DCI*, vol. 1/4 p. 17; vol. 2/4 p. 21. et seq., with an analysis of an interesting decision of the <u>District Court of Tel Aviv re Eitan v. Israel Discount Bank</u>

[26] Sassoon, *Letter of Credit in Kaplan*, Israeli Business Law, The Hague, London, Boston 1996, p. 311 et seq.; Sassoon, 'Akkreditive', in *Kaplan/Elmaleh*, Israelisches Wirtschaftsrecht, Munich, Vienna 1998, p. 109 et seq.

[27] Discussed by Sassoon, *Letters of Credit in Kaplan*, Israeli Business law, The Hague, London, Boston 1996, p. 312.

Kuwait

General Remarks

Articles 367 to 377 of the Kuwaiti Commercial Code[28] deal with the law of documentary credits (al-i'timâd almustanadi)[29]. This demonstrates the great importance of documentary credits in Arab countries. According to Carlson[30] documentary credits are used in 90% of all trading transactions for securing purchase prices.

Kuwait does not base its law on the Lebanese documentary credit law principles as implemented in many other Arab jurisdictions, but has created its own system of statutory provisions based on the UCP[31].

Commercial Code

Article 367

1. The documentary credit is an agreement by which the bank undertakes to issue a credit upon a customer's (the applicant's) request for the benefit of a third party (the beneficiary) which is guaranteed by documents that represent transported goods or goods ready for transport.

2. The documentary credit shall be independent from the contract for which it is issued. The bank shall remain alien to such contract.

---

[28] Law No. 68/1980
[29] See Schütze, 'Bankgarantien und Dokumentenakkreditive im deutsch-arabischen Handelsverkehr', in: von Boehmer, *Deutsche Unternehmen in den Golfstaaten*, 1990, p. 277 et seq. (289).
[30] See Carlson, *Legal Issues and Negotiation in Islamic Banking and Finance*, 1986, p. 67 et seq. (79).
[31] See the explanatory memorandum on the Commercial Code 1980, *Law Bulletin* No. 1338 of 19 January 1981, p. 81 et seq. (105).

Article 368

The documents against which payments, acceptance or discounting are to be made shall be specified in the request to issue the documentary credit, its confirmation or notification.

Article 369

If the documents comply with the terms and conditions of the documentary credit, the issuing bank shall effect payment, acceptance or discounting as provided for in the credit.

Article 370

1. The documentary credit may be confirmed or revocable.

2. The credit opening contract shall define expressly the type of the credit. In the absence of such express definition the credit shall be deemed revocable.

Article 371

The revocable credit does not create an obligation of the bank to the beneficiary. The bank may modify or cancel the credit at all times, either at its own initiative or the applicant's request, without being required to notify the beneficiary, provided that the modification or cancellation is done in good faith and in a reasonable time.

Article 372

1. By an irrevocable credit the bank undertakes a direct and definite obligation to the beneficiary or any good-faith holder of the documents specified in the application to issue the credit.

2. An irrevocable documentary credit may not be cancelled or modified unless all concerned parties agree.

3. An irrevocable credit may be confirmed by another bank which then undertakes a direct and definite obligation to the beneficiary.

4. The simple notification of opening a documentary credit forwarded to the beneficiary via another bank shall not be deemed a confirmation of the credit.

Article 373

1. An irrevocable documentary credit shall contain an expiry date for its validity by which the documents need to be presented to effect payment, acceptance or discounting.

2. If the expiry date of the credit's validity falls on a bank holiday the validity period shall be extended to the first working day following the bank holiday.

3. Except for bank holidays, the credit's validity shall not be extended even if the expiry date falls in a period during which the bank's business is interrupted by *force majeure*, unless the applicant expressly agrees to an extension.

Article 374

1. The bank shall examine whether the documents comply with the instructions of the applicant of the credit.

2. If the bank refuses the documents it shall immediately notify the beneficiary by specifying the reasons for refusal.

Article 375

1. The bank does not assume any liability if the presented documents on their face appear to comply with the applicant's instructions.

2. The bank shall not be liable for the performance of consignors and insurers of the goods for which payment the credit has been issued, their quality, weight, condition, packaging or value.

Article 376

The documentary credit may not be assigned in part or in whole unless the issuing bank is authorized by the applicant to make payment on the credit in accordance with the applicant's instructions in part or in full to one or several third parties. The credit may not be assigned unless the concerned bank agrees to the assignment. The credit may be assigned only once unless otherwise agreed upon.

Article 377

If the applicant does not pay to the bank the value of the consignment documents according to the terms of the credit within three months running from the date of notification to the applicant that the documents have been presented, the bank may sell the goods in accordance with the execution proceedings applicable to commercially pledged property.

Libya

General Remarks

Libyan laws do not contain any particular statute on documentary credits. Documentary transactions, however, are comprehensively governed in Articles 114, 249 et seq. of the Commercial Code. Although Libyan laws are in many respects based on Egyptian laws, the quoted Articles are influenced by Italian law.

Commercial Code

Article 114 [Payment through a bank]

When payment of the price is to be made through a bank the vendor cannot make any claim against the purchaser when the bank has refused to make payment, and if such refusal has been recorded in due form as required by customs at the presentation of documents.

A bank which has confirmed the credit to the vendor can only raise objections that are based on the incompleteness or irregularity of documents or relating to the due confirmation of the credit.

Article 249 [Rights upon presentation of documents]

The holder of a documentary credit is entitled to the rights provided for in the documentary credit upon presentation of the documents on the condition that he is in the lawful possession thereof.

A debtor who performs under the documentary credit in good faith or without gross negligence is discharged even if the holder is not the owner of the right.

Article 250 [Value of document]

If a document indicates its nominal value in figures or numbers it shall be valid despite a discrepancy having the amount spelled out in words. If the amount is spelled out several times in figures or in words the smaller amount shall be prevailing.

Article 251 [Allowed defences of the debtor]

A debtor may raise against the holder of the document only personal or formal defences, defences explicitly stated in the document, forging of the debtor's signature, defects in legal capacity or representation at the time of issuance, or the absence of any conditions necessary for exercising the claim.

A debtor may not raise defences against the holder of the document based on personal relations with previous holders unless the holder acted deliberately to the detriment of the debtor at the time of acquiring the document.

Article 252 [Possession of the document in good faith]

If the holder of a documentary credit acquired possession of the document in good faith and in accordance with the provisions on its transfer it cannot be subject to a claim of surrender.

Article 253 [Transfer of rights attached to the document]

The transfer of the documentary credit includes all ancillary rights attached to the documentary credit.

Article 254 [Documents representing goods]

A document that represents goods entitles its holder to demand delivery of the goods specified therein, to obtain possession of them and to trade them by transferring the document.

Article 255 [Registration of liens on the document]

Pledges, attachments, seizures and any other charges on the rights arising from a credit or on the goods represented thereby are invalid unless they are registered in the document.

Article 256 [Right to use the documents]

In the case of a right to credit documents, the rights of the beneficiary include premiums and any other benefits incurred by the document.

Premiums shall be invested so that they result in gains, and the right of use extends to such gain. If the parties do not agree on the method of investments, the juridical authority shall determine them.

A pledge of a credit document does not extend to premiums or any other ancillary benefits of the document.

Article 257 [Conversion of registered and bearer documents]

Credit documents made out to their holder may be converted by the issuing party into registered documents at the request and at the expense of their holder. Registered documents may be converted into bearer documents at the request and at the expense of the party in whose name they are registered unless the issuer explicitly excluded the documents' convertibility. Such party shall prove its identity and its legal capacity by a notarial certificate.

Article 258 [Multiple documents and division]

Credit documents issued in a series may be combined in one aggregate at the request and at the expense of the holder, and aggregate documents may be divided.

Article 259 [Applicable laws]

The provisions of this book apply unless other provisions of the Code or specific laws provide otherwise. Public credit documents, paper money and other equivalent documents are governed by specific provisions.

Article 260 [Exempted documents]

The provisions of this chapter do not apply to documents whose only purpose is to identify the party entitled to performance or to permit the transfer of a right without observance of the due forms for an assignment.

Article 261 [Rights of a holder]

The transfer of a bearer document is effected by handing it over. The holder of a bearer document is entitled to exercise the right arising therefrom upon presentation of the document.

Article 262 [Documents with financial obligations]

Credit documents that provide for an obligation to pay a sum of money may only be issued to bearers as provided for by law.

Article 263 [Substitution of damaged documents]

The holder of a damaged document which is no longer suitable for circulation but identifiable with certainty is entitled to demand from the issuing party an equivalent document against restitution of the first document and reimbursement of expenses.

Article 264 [Cancellation of lost documents]

Notwithstanding provisions of special laws, the cancellation of lost or purloined bearer documents is not permitted.

The person who notifies the issuing party that a bearer share has been lost or purloined and provides proof thereof is entitled to performance and to ancillary rights after the period stipulated by the document has expired.

A debtor who carries out performance in favour of the holder of the document prior to said date is discharged from his obligation unless it can be evidenced that the debtor had knowledge that its possession by the presenting party was fraudulent.

If the lost or purloined documents are bearer shares the applicant may be authorized by a court to exercise the rights attached to the shares prior to the stipulated date until the documents are retrieved. If it is considered necessary the applicant shall deposit a security prior to exercising rights. The applicant's rights, if any, against the holder of the documents remain unaffected.

Article 265 [Destruction of a document]

The holder of a bearer document who proves that the document was destroyed may demand a duplicate or an equivalent document from the issuing party. The expenses shall be borne by the applicant. If the destruction of the document cannot be evidenced the proceeding article shall apply.

Article 266 [Lawful possession]

The holder of a document to order is entitled to exercise the right mentioned therein if there is a continuous series of endorsements.

Article 267 [Validity of an endorsement]

An endorsement must be written on the document and signed by the endorser. The endorsement is valid even if it does not indicate the name of the endorsee. An endorsement to bearer is valid as a blank endorsement.

Article 268 [Unconditional nature of an endorsement]

A condition of whatever nature that has been added to an endorsement shall be treated as if it were not written. A partial endorsement is invalid.

Article 269 [Effects of the endorsement]

An endorsement transfers all rights attached to the document.

If the document bears a blank endorsement the holder may fill in its own name or the name of another party or endorse the document again or assign it to a third party without completing the blank endorsement or affixing a new endorsement.

Article 270 [Liability of an endorser for fulfilment]

Notwithstanding any contrary legal provisions or any contrary clause of the document an endorser is not liable for default of performance by the issuing party.

Article 271 [Endorsement for collection]

If a clause is added to an endorsement which provides for a collection right, an endorsee may exercise all rights attached to the document; the endorsee cannot, however, endorse the document except by virtue of a power of attorney.

The issuing party may use against the endorsee by virtue of a power of attorney only the defences which may be used against the endorser.

The validity of an endorsement written by virtue of a power of attorney does not cease by the death or by the subsequent legal incapacity of the endorser.

Article 272 [Endorsement for guarantee purposes]

If an endorsement is supplemented by a pledge or other security the endorsee may exercise all rights attached to the document. An endorsement made by the endorsee is only valid as an endorsement by virtue of a power of attorney.

An issuing party cannot defend itself against the endorsee by virtue of a defence based on its personal relations with the endorser unless the endorsee, on receiving the document, deliberately acted to the detriment of the issuing party.

Article 273 [Acquisition without endorsement]

The transfer of a document to order by any other way than by endorsement triggers the effect of an assignment.

Article 274 [Cancellation of lost or purloined documents]

If a document has been lost, purloined or destroyed the holder may notify the debtor and apply for cancellation of the document to the president of the court at the place of payment.

The application must indicate the essential terms of the documents and in case of a blank document such prerequisites that are sufficient to identify the document.

After the president of the court has verified the facts and the right of the holder, it declares the cancellation by an order and authorizes payment of the document thirty days from the date of publication of the order in the Official Gazette, provided that no objection has as yet been filed by the holder. If the document is not due, the period for the payment shall run until the due date.

The court order shall be notified to the debtor and published in the Official Gazette by the applicant.

Notwithstanding the notice the debtor shall be discharged by a payment made to the holder prior to the notification of the order.

Article 275 [Procedure for objection]

An objection by a holder must be filed with the court which declared the cancellation by a writ to be served on the applicant and the debtor. An objection is not admissible without depositing the document at the registry of the tribunal.

If an objection is rejected the document shall be handed over to the party who has applied for the cancellation order.

Article 276 [Precautionary measures]

During the period prescribed for the cancellation of the lost, purloined or destroyed document the applicant may carry out any acts necessary to preserve its rights and if the document is due or if it is payable at sight the applicant may demand payment thereof against security or request that the amount is paid to the court.

Article 277 [Expiration of the time limit without objection]

After the period for cancellation has expired without any objection being raised, the document ceases to be valid, without prejudice to the claims of a holder against the party who applied for the cancellation.

Libya

The party who applied for the cancellation may demand payment on presentation of the order and of a certificate by the court's registrar attesting that no objection has been raised.

If the document was issued as a blank document or if it is not yet due, the applicant may obtain a duplicate.

Article 278 [Applicability of special laws]

The foregoing provisions are applicable to documents to order and subject to special laws if they are consistent with them.

Article 279 [Right under a registered document]

The holder of a registered document is entitled to exercise the rights mentioned therein if he is named in the document and in the register of the issuing party.

Article 280 [Transfer of registered documents]

The transfer of registered documents is effected by the registration the acquirer's name in the document and in the register of the issuing party or by the issuing of a new document made out to the name of the new holder. The issuance of the new document is evidenced by the inscription in the register.

Whoever demands the document to be made out in the name of another person or the issuance of a new document to be made out to another person has to prove his identity and his right of disposition by way of a certificate issued by a notary or a stockbroker. If the registration of the issuance is requested by the acquirer the latter has to produce the documents and to prove his authority by means of an authentic act.

The registration in the register and on the document shall be made by and at the responsibility of the issuing party.

If the issuing party carries out the transfer in the manner indicated in this article, it shall be exempted from any responsibilities except in case of fault.

Article 281 [Transfer of registered documents by endorsement]

Unless otherwise provided for by legal provisions, a registered document may also be transferred by an endorsement certified by a notary or stockbroker.

An endorsement must be dated and signed by the endorser and include the name of the endorsee. If the document is not fully paid the signature of the endorsee is also required.

A transfer by endorsement is only effective for the issuing party after it has been registered in the register. An endorsee who proves that he is the holder of the document by virtue of a continuous series of endorsements is entitled to request the registration of the transfer in the register of the issuing party.

Article 282 [Encumbrances of the document]

No encumbrance of the rights indicated in the document has an impact on the issuing party and any third parties unless it is registered in the document and in the register and made by way of a certificate by a notary in accordance with foregoing provisions.

Article 283 [Right of use]

If a person has the right to make use of the claims included in a registered document he is entitled to demand a separate document from the owner.

Article 284 [Pledge]

A pledge over a registered document may be effected by delivery of the document, endorsed with the clause "as security" or another equivalent clause.

The endorsee of an endorsement for security purposes may not transfer the document to any party except by an endorsement by virtue of a power of attorney.

Article 285 [Cancellation and cancellation procedure]

If the document is lost, purloined or destroyed the registered holder or an endorsee of the document may notify such fact to the issuing party and demand the cancellation of the document in accordance with the provisions relating to documents to order.

If a registered share is lost, purloined or destroyed the applicant may, during the period for cancellation, exercise any rights attached to the share, subject to the deposit of a security if such security is necessary.

The final order of cancellation invalidates the document but does not prejudice any claims of a holder against the party who has obtained the new document.

Malaysia

General Remarks

Although Malaysian law does not provide for statutory rules explicitly addressing documentary credits, there is comprehensive jurisprudence and legal literature[32], offering a wide range of answers to the questions involved[33]. Most issues are addressed by applying principles established by English courts. Conflicts arise from the application of the Islamic Banking Act of 1983[34]. To meet the specific requirements of Islamic law three types of documentary credits have been developed[35]:

- Documentary credits under the principle of Al-Wakalah (agency)
- Documentary credits under the principle of Al-Musyarakah (partnership)
- Documentary credits under the principle of Al-Murabahah (cost-plus)

If the applicant requests that a letter of credit be issued under the principle of Al-Wakalah, the bank may ask the customer to deposit the amount of the credit with the bank. The bank then forwards the deposited amount to the negotiating bank and subsequently hands over the documents to the applicant. The services of the bank are compensated for by a fee and a commission.

Under the principle of Al-Musyarakah, the bank and the applicant jointly participate in the credit. The applicant deposits a portion of the amount of the credit with the bank and the remainder is financed by the bank in its own name. Upon payment of the credit and release of the documents the applicant sells the goods

---

[32] For references, see Myist Soe, *The Law of Banking in Singapore & Malaysia*, 1997, p. 339 et seq.

[33] Re: prevailing practice, see Abdul Latift Abdul Rahim, *DCI*, vol. 2/1 p. 16.

[34] Re: specific problems, see Illiayas, *Islamic Interest-Free Banking in Malaysia: Some Legal Considerations* (1955), 3 Mal.L.J. cxlix; Klötzel, Islamic Banking in Malaysia, *Festschrift für Schütze*, 1999, p. 381 et seq.

[35] See El Tayeb, *Legal Principles of Documentary Credits*, 1998, p. 46 et seq.

in accordance with the terms agreed with the bank in the credit opening agreement. The applicant and the bank share the profits resulting from the sale of the goods in accordance with the agreed ratios. Under the principle of Al-Musyarakah the bank would also participate in any losses incurred by the credit transaction[36].

A credit opened under the principle of Al-Murabahah stipulates that the bank must purchase the goods at the request of the applicant, who promises to buy the goods from the bank once the bank has received them. The sales price agreed between the bank and the applicant includes the bank's costs and a profit margin.

---

[36] Klötzel, Islamic Banking in Malaysia, *Festschrift für Schütze*, 1999, p. 387

Mexico

General Remarks

The Mexican law on documentary credits is included in Articles 311 to 320 of the Commercial Code 1932[37]. These provisions govern documentary credits in a rather obsolete form.

Commercial Code

Article 311

Credits must be issued for the benefit of a specific person and shall not be negotiable. A credit shall contain a fixed amount or variable indefinite partial amounts, which shall add up to a maximum amount which shall be precisely indicated.

Article 312

Credits shall neither be accepted nor protested and shall not vest any rights in their holder against any person to whom they are addressed.

Article 313

The holder has no rights against the applicant except if the amount of the credit is in the possession of the applicant or if the holder is the creditor of this amount. In these cases the applicant shall be liable to pay the amount of the credit if the credit is not paid and to pay damages. If the holder of the credit granted a guaranty or insured the amount of the credit and the credit is not paid, the applicant is liable for payment of damages.

Damages within the meaning of this Article shall not exceed 1/10 of the amount which has not been paid plus costs incurred by the insurance or the guaranty.

---

[37] See Barrera Graf, *Estudios de derecho mercantil*, 1958.

Article 314

The issuing entity may cancel the credit at any time by informing the holder of the credit and the person to whom the credit is addressed, except if the holder of the credit has possession of the credit's amount, has insured the credit's amount or provided a guaranty, or if the holder is the creditor of such amount.

Article 315

The applicant remains liable to the issuing entity for the amount which such entity paid according to the credit's limits.

Article 316

Unless otherwise agreed, the term of credit shall be six months from the date of its issuance. If the date provided for in the credit or the period provided for in this article expires, the letter of credit shall terminate.

Article 317

The confirmed credit is a direct liability of the issuing entity for the third party; it is required to be in writing and may not be revoked by the applicant.

Article 318

Unless otherwise provided for, the third party for whose benefit the credit has been issued may transfer the credit. However, the beneficiary remains bound to all obligations stipulated by the confirmation of the credit.

Article 319

The issuing entity shall be liable to the applicant according to the laws on professional mandates. It shall be liable for the actions of persons appointed by it for the consummation of the transaction, unless otherwise agreed.

Article 320

The issuing entity may raise any objections against the third party beneficiary which result from the confirmation of the credit and all alterations of the relationship between the third party and the applicant. In no event may it raise objections which result from the relationship between the applicant and the issuing entity itself.

Oman

General Remarks

Articles 377 through 387 include the Omani laws on documentary credits[38].

Commercial Code

Article 377

A documentary credit is a contract by which a bank undertakes to issue a credit upon one of its customer's requests (the applicant of the credit) for the benefit of another party (the beneficiary) which is secured by documents representing shipped goods or goods ready for shipment.

The documentary credit shall be separate from the contract for which the credit has been issued and the bank shall remain alien to such contract.

Article 378

The request for the issuance of a documentary credit, confirmation or notification shall precisely define the documents against which payment, acceptance or discounting are to be made.

Article 379

The issuing bank shall be obligated to effect payment, acceptance and discounting as agreed in the credit opening contract if the documents comply with the details and terms set forth in the credit opening contract.

Article 380

A documentary credit may be revocable or irrevocable.
The credit opening contract shall contain an express specification as to the type of credit. In the absence of such specification the credit shall be deemed revocable.

---

[38] Law No. 55/1990

Article 381

A revocable documentary credit does not constitute an obligation by the bank to the beneficiary. The bank may modify or cancel the credit at its own initiative or at the applicant's request at any time and without being required to notify the beneficiary thereof, provided that a modification or cancellation is made in good faith and at a reasonable time.

Article 382

If the documentary credit is irrevocable, the bank undertakes a definite and direct obligation to the beneficiary and any *bona fide* holder of documents drawn according to the agreement for which the credit was issued.

An irrevocable documentary credit may not be cancelled or modified unless all concerned parties agree.

An irrevocable credit may be confirmed by another bank which thereby undertakes a direct and definite obligation to the beneficiary.

The simple advice that an irrevocable documentary credit has been issued to the beneficiary through another bank shall not be considered a confirmation of the credit by such bank.

Article 383

An irrevocable documentary credit shall contain an expiry date for its validity and the presentation of documents to effect payment, acceptance or discounting.

If the designated expiry date for the validity of the credit falls on a day which is a bank holiday, the validity period shall be extended to the first working day following that holiday.

Except for holidays, the validity of the credit shall not be extended if the expiry date occurs during an interruption of the bank's business caused by *force majeure*, unless the applicant gives express instruction to the contrary.

Article 384

The bank shall examine if the documents comply with the instructions given by the applicant.

If the bank refuses to take up the documents it shall promptly notify the applicant therefor and explain the reasons for its refusal.

Article 385

The bank shall not be liable if the presented documents on their face appear to comply with the instructions by the applicant.

The bank shall not assume any liability for the specifications of the goods for which payment the credit was issued, their quality, weight, condition, packing or value and for the obligations to the consignors and insurers.

Article 386

A credit may not be assigned or fractioned unless the issuing bank is authorized by the applicant to make payment in full or in part according to instructions by the beneficiary to one or several persons other than the beneficiary.

Unless otherwise agreed, the credit may be assigned only upon express agreement by the bank and only once.

Article 387

If the applicant does not reimburse the bank for the value of transport documents complying with the terms of the credit within three months of receiving notice of presentation of such documents, the bank may sell the goods according to procedures elected by the court.

Qatar

General Remarks

The Quatrain law on documentary credits is based on the rudimentary Lebanese law in the Commercial Code of 1971.

Commercial Code[39]

Article 348

If the credit provides for a payment in favour of a third party and the bank confirms such credit to the beneficiary, it may not subsequently revoke or modify the credit without the beneficiary's consent.

The bank shall be entitled to reimbursement of all sums paid and expenses incurred in the performance of the requested service plus agreed interest and, in the absence of an agreement, to legal interest calculated as of the date of payment. The bank may also charge a commission.

---

[39] Law No. 16/1971.

Russia

General Remarks

The Russian law on documentary credits[40] is governed by Articles 867 to 873 of part II of the Civil Code. The Russian courts interpret the statutory provisions in accordance with the UCP 500[41]. On 1 November 2001 the Regulation by the Central Bank of Russia concerning clearing settlements in the Russian Federation was handed down, which governs the handling of documentary letters of credit operations in chapters 4 to 6[42]. This Regulation has not come into effect yet, since it has not been registered with the Russian Federation's Ministry of Justice.

Both the Regulation of the Russian Central Bank and the Civil Code provide for some requirements that are unusual in international documentary credit practice. In some instances these even conflict with provisions of the UCP 500. Unlike the UCP 500, the Russian law stipulates that documentary credits are revocable unless otherwise agreed. Under Russian law the nominated bank is responsible for verifying the genuineness of signatures and seals. Russian law does include provisions regarding the transfer of documentary credits, and banks have expressed concerns when requested to open a transferable documentary credit. Even if Russian banks subject documentary credits to the UCP 500, particularities of Russian law might be applied.

The Russian law on documentary credits[43] is governed by Articles 867 to 873 of part II of the Civil Code. Unless otherwise agreed, documentary credits are revocable. The Russian courts interpret the statutory provisions in accordance with the UCP 500[44].

---

[40] For practical issues, see: Kobakzhidze, *DCI*, vol. 1/1 p. 21, vol. 1/3 p. 16, vol. 2/1 p. 16, vol. 2/3 p. 18, vol. 3/2 p. 18, vol. 4/2 p. 22, vol. 5/1 p. 14, vol. 6/3 p. 18, which highlights practical difficulties of confirmations of documentary credits by Russian banks.

[41] See Kobakzhidze, *DCI*, vol. 5/4, p. 18.

[42] For details, see: Kobakzhidze, *DCI*, vol. 7/1, p. 21.

[43] For practical issues, see: Kobakzhidze, *DCI*, vol. 1/1 p. 21, vol. 1/3 p. 16, vol. 2/1 p. 16, vol. 2/3 p. 18, vol. 3/2 p. 18, vol. 4/2 p. 22, vol. 5/1 p. 14, vol. 6/3 p. 18, which highlights practical difficulties of confirmations of documentary credits by Russian banks.

[44] See Kobakzhidze, *DCI*, vol. 5/4, p. 18.

Civil Code

§3 PAYMENTS BY LETTER OF CREDIT

Article 867 [General provisions on payment by letter of credit]

1. If payments are made by letter of credit, the bank that is authorized by the payer to open the letter of credit (the issuing bank) in accordance with the payer's order is obligated to make payments to the beneficiary or to pay, accept, or honour a transfer bill of exchange or authorize another bank (the executing bank) to make payments to the beneficiary, or to pay, accept or honour a transfer bill of exchange.

   The rules that apply to the executing bank shall also apply to an emitting bank that has made payments to the beneficiary or has paid, accepted, or honoured a transfer bill of exchange, respectively.

2. If a covered (deposited) letter of credit is opened, the issuing bank is obligated upon the opening of the letter of credit to transfer the amount of the letter of credit (coverage), at the payer's expense or of the credit provided to the payer, to the executing bank for the entire term of the issuing bank's obligation.

   If a non-covered (guaranteed) letter of credit is opened, the executing bank is entitled to deduct the total amount of the letter of credit from the account of the issuing bank held by the executing bank.

3. The procedure for making settlements under a letter of credit shall be governed by a statute and also by bank rules set up in accordance with such statute and rules and by customs of trade applied in banking practice.

Article 868 [Revocable letter of credit]

1. A revocable letter of credit is a letter of credit that may be modified or revoked by the issuing bank without prior notice to the beneficiary. The revocation of the letter of credit does not result in any obligation of the issuing bank to the beneficiary.

2. The executing bank is obligated to make payment or other operations under a revocable letter of credit unless it has received notice of the change of conditions or the revocation of the letter of credit prior to making such payment.

3. A letter of credit is revocable unless its wording expressly provides otherwise.

Russia

Article 869 [Irrevocable Letter of Credit]

1. An irrevocable letter of credit is a letter of credit that may not be revoked without the beneficiary's consent.

2. Upon the issuing bank's request, the executing bank involved in the transaction of a letter of credit operation may guarantee an irrevocable letter of credit (guaranteed letter of credit). Such a guaranty constitutes acceptance by the executing bank of an obligation that exists in addition to the issuing bank's obligation to make payment in accordance with the terms of the letter of credit.

   An irrevocable letter of credit that is guaranteed by the executing bank may not be modified or revoked without the executing bank's consent.

Article 870 [Execution of a letter of credit]

1. In order to execute a letter of credit the beneficiary shall present to the executing bank documents evidencing due performance of all conditions of the letter of credit. If any – even if only one – condition of the letter of credit is not met, the letter of credit shall not be executed.

2. If the executing bank has made payment of another operation in connection with the terms of the letter of credit, the issuing bank shall compensate it for the incurred expenditures. These expenses and all of the issuing bank's other expenditures related to the execution of the letter of credit shall be compensated by the payer.

Article 871 [Refusal to accept documents]

1. If the executing bank refuses to accept documents that by evident features do not correspond to the terms of the letter of credit, it shall inform the beneficiary and the issuing bank promptly and indicate the reasons for refusal.

2. If the issuing bank, after receipt of the documents accepted by the executing bank, concludes that they do not correspond by evident features to the terms of the letter of credit, it is entitled to refuse acceptance and to demand repayment of the amount paid to the beneficiary from the executing bank as a violation of the terms of the letter of credit and, in case of an uncovered letter of credit, to refuse compensation of the disbursed amounts.

Article 872 [Liability for violation of the terms of a letter of credit]

1. The issuing bank shall be liable to the payer and the executing bank to the issuing bank for a violation of the terms of the letter of credit, except for the cases provided in this Article.

2. In case of unjustified refusal by the executing bank to make payment under a covered or guaranteed letter of credit the executing bank shall be liable to the beneficiary.

3. In case of making an incorrect payment by the executing bank under a covered or guaranteed letter of credit as a result of violations of the terms of the letter of credit, the payer shall be liable to the executing bank.

Article 873 [Termination of a Letter of Credit]

1. The executing bank's liability under a letter of credit shall terminate
   - upon expiry of the term of the letter of credit;
   - upon a statement by the beneficiary of its decision not to use the letter of credit during its term of effectiveness, if this is permitted by the terms of the letter of credit;
   - on demand by the payer for the full or partial cancellation of the letter of credit, if such cancellation is permitted under the terms of the letter of credit.

   The executing bank shall inform the issuing bank of the termination of the letter of credit.

2. The unused amount of a covered letter of credit shall be returned to the issuing bank promptly at the time of the termination of the letter of credit. The issuing bank is obligated to transfer the returned amount to the payer's account from which the funds were debited.

Russia

Singapore

General Remarks

There are no statutory provisions on documentary credits in Singapore law. Nevertheless, comprehensive legal literature[45] is available that is based on English law principles of documentary credits.

Jurisprudence has mainly dealt with strict compliance and the risk of fraud. In the case Union Overseas Bank v. Chua Teng Hwee[46] a "certificate of weight" was presented instead of the required certificate of inspection. The court confirmed the principle of strict compliance and regarded the documents as not complying with the terms of the documentary credit. The further decisions in Bhojwani and Anor v. Chung Khiaw Bank Ltd[47], Amixco, Asia (Pte) Ltd v. Bumiputra Malaysia Bhd.[48], Lambias Co. Pte Ltd v. HSBC[49] and Ringler Pte Ltd v. United Commercial Bank[50] also confirm the application of the principle of strict compliance in Singapore law.

In the case African Commercial Corporation v. Hussainali[51] the court rejected the bank's objection that the goods were defective as irrelevant. The court confirmed the general principle that the issuing bank shall only examine the regularity of the documents but may not examine the underlying transaction.

In the case Gian Singh and Co. Ltd v. Bank de l'Indochine[52] the court stated that the risk of fraud was to be borne by the applicant. Consequently, the issuing bank is entitled to demand reimbursement of the paid credit amount from the applicant.

---

[45] Chew Choon Teck, *Strict Compliance in Letter of Credit: The Banker's Protection or Bane?* (1990) 2 S.Ac.L.J. 70; Ellinger, *Documentary Letters of Credit*, 1970; *The Tender of Fraudulent Documents under Documentary Letters of Credit* (1965) 7 Mal.L.R. 24; *Strict Compliance with the Term of a Documentary Credit - O.U.B. v. Chuang Teng Hwee* (1964) 6 Mal.L.R.417; Myint Soe, *The Law of Banking in Singapore and Malaysia*, 1997, p. 339 et seq.; Poh Chu Chai, *Law of Banking*, vol. 2, 3rd ed. 1995, S. 467 et seq.; Teoh Oon Teong, *Letter of Credit: A Conflict of Laws Perspective*, (1990) 2 S.Sc.L.J.51.
[46] (1964) 6 Mal. L.J. 165.
[47] (1990) 3 Mal.L.J. 260; see Myint Soe, *The Law of Banking in Singapore & Malaysia*, 1997, p. 354 et seq.
[48] (1992) 2 S.L.R. 943.
[49] (1993) 2 S.L.R. 751.
[50] (1995) 1 S.L.R. 389.
[51] (1959) M.L.J. 125.
[52] (1974) 1 Lloyds Rep. 56 (first instance judgment) (1972) 1 M.L.J. 146.

Slovakia

General Remarks

The Slovakian law on documentary credits is governed in §§682 to 691 of the Commercial Code. The provisions correspond to the provisions applicable in the Czech Republic.

Commercial Code

§682 [Basic provisions]

1. By the agreement on the issuance of a credit, the bank becomes liable to the applicant to make a specified payment to a third party (beneficiary) according to the applicant's instructions and for his account if the beneficiary meets the stipulated conditions by a specified time; the applicant undertakes to pay the bank a fee.

2. The agreement must be in writing.

§683 [Issuance of the credit]

1. The bank notifies the beneficiary in compliance with the agreement that a credit has been issued for his benefit and informs the beneficiary of the credit's terms. The credit document shall include the payment which the bank undertakes to make, the term of the credit and the credit's conditions, which the beneficiary has to meet within such term so that the beneficiary may demand payment from the bank.

2. After execution of the agreement the bank shall make the notification according to subsection 1 without undue delay unless the agreement indicates that the notification shall only be made upon instruction by the applicant.

3. The bank's liability to the beneficiary becomes existent by the notification according to subsection 1.

4. The liability of the applicant to the bank becomes existent upon issuance of the credit.

5. The credit document may provide in particular for the bank's liability to pay a specified amount or to accept a draft.

Slovakia

§684 [Amount of the fee]

If no fee for the issuance of the credit has been agreed upon the applicant shall pay the fee that is customary at the time of the execution of the agreement.

LEGAL STATUS OF THE BANK TO THE BENEFICIARY

§685 [Undertaking by the bank]

The undertaking by the bank of the letter of credit is independent from the relationship between the applicant and the beneficiary.

§686 [Revocable and irrevocable credits]

1. If the credit document does not provide for the revocability of the credit the bank may only amend or revoke the credit upon approval of the applicant and the beneficiary.

2. If the credit document provides for revocability, the bank may amend or revoke the credit with effect for the beneficiary as long as the conditions of the credit are not met.

3. The amendment or revocation of a credit can only be made in writing.

§687 [Additional banks]

1. If an irrevocable credit was confirmed by another bank upon the issuing bank's instruction the beneficiary's claim to performance against such bank arises at the time such bank confirms the credit to the beneficiary. The issuing bank and the bank which confirms the credit are jointly and severally liable to the beneficiary.

2. A letter of credit confirmed by a second bank can only be amended or revoked upon such bank's approval.

3. If the bank which confirms the credit honours the credit in compliance with the credit's terms such bank has a claim for performance against the issuing bank.

§688 [Liability for incorrect notification]

If the issuance of the credit is accomplished through another bank such bank is liable for the damage that results from the incorrectness of the notification. However, such bank is not liable for the credit itself.

DOCUMENTARY CREDIT

§689 [Commitment by the bank]

If all documents referred to in the documentary credit are presented to the bank during the credit's lifetime the bank shall be committed to the beneficiary to perform.

§690 [Strict compliance]

1. The bank undertakes to examine the compliance of the presented documents with the conditions set forth by the credit with adequate diligence.

2. The bank shall be liable to the applicant for the loss or destruction of the documents taken over by the beneficiary unless the damage could not have been avoided if adequate diligence was applied.

§691

The provisions of §§689 to 690 apply *mutadis mutandis* to credits which provide for a claim for performance under conditions other than the presentation of the documents.

Slovakia

Sudan

Sudan

General Remarks

The laws of Sudan do not include specific provisions on documentary credits. Nor does the Civil Transactions Act of 1984 contain specific rules on documentary credits. The Encyclopaedia of Islamic Banking contains three theories of documentary credits[53] which also apply in Sudanese law: the agency theory, the assignment theory and the guarantee theory. According to El Tayeb[54] the documentary credit qualifies as a modern law agreement to the extent that the obligations under the documentary credit do not conflict with Islamic law, e.g., with regard to interest.

---

[53] See El Tayeb, *Legal Principles of Documentary Credits*, 1998, p. 42 et seq., with further references.
[54] See El Tayeb, id., p. 42.

Switzerland

General Remarks

Swiss law does not contain provisions specifically dealing with documentary credits[55]. The Swiss Supreme Court applies the laws of the domicile of the issuing bank to their undertakings and the laws of the domicile of the confirming bank to their undertakings[56]. The Swiss courts acknowledge the principles of strict compliance and the independence between credit and trade transactions. Fraud clearly sets a limit to the banks' undertakings resulting from the credit[57], and the applicant may prevent payment of the credit by way of injunction against the beneficiary. However, Swiss law does not acknowledge the right to prevent reimbursement of the confirming bank or the payment agent unless such correspondent bank collaborates with the deceiving beneficiary[58].

---

[55] See the general literature: Gafner, *Das Dokumenten-Akkreditiv nach schweizerischem Recht und dem internationalen Regulativ von 1933*, Berne 1948; Hahn, *Die Übertragung von Dokumentenakkreditiven*, Fribourg 1968; Keller, *L'accréditif documentaire en droit suisse*, Geneva 1941; Lombardini, *Droit et pratique du crédit documentaire*, Zurich 1994; Schärrer, *Die Rechtsstellung des Begünstigten im Dokumentenakkreditiv*, Berne 1980; Ulrich, *Rechtsprobleme des Dokumentenakkreditivs*, Zurich 1989; Hartmann, *Der Akkreditiv-Eröffnungsauftrag nach den einheitlichen Richtlinien und Gebräuchen für Dokumentenakkreditive (Revision 1962) und nach schweizerischem Recht*, Zürich 1974; also see Lombardini, *DCI*, vol. 3/1, p. 20, on the current practice.

[56] Federal Court BGE 115 II, 67 commented by Dilger RIW 1990, 324 et seq.; Hartmann, *Der Akkreditiv-Eröffnungsauftrag nach den einheitlichen Richtlinien und Gebräuchen für Dokumentenakkreditive (Revision 1962) und nach schweizerischem Recht,* Zurich 1974, p. 49.

[57] Federal Court BGE 115 II, 67; Eschmann, *Der einstweilige Rechtsschutz des Akkreditivs-Auftraggeber in Deutschland, England und der Schweiz,* 1994.

[58] Gutzwiller, *Bemerkungen zum Verhältnis zwischen Akkreditivbank und Korrespondenzbank*, SchweizJZ 1984, p. 162.

Syria

General Remarks

The Syrian provisions on documentary credits are based on Lebanese law and are included in Article 408 of the Syrian Commercial Code[59].

Commercial Code

Article 408

1. If a bank credit has been effected to make a payment for the benefit of a third party and such credit has been confirmed by the bank to the beneficiary, the credit may no longer be revoked or modified without the beneficiary's consent. The bank is directly and definitely liable to the third party for making the payment.

2. The bank is entitled to demand reimbursement of the paid amounts and expenses made for the execution of its mandate, to interest as agreed, or in the absence of an agreement, statutory interest from the day of the payment.

3. It is equally entitled to a commission.

---

[59] Law No. 149/1949.

Tunisia

General Comments

The Tunisian laws on documentary credits[60] are included in Articles 720 to 727 of the Commercial Code of 1959.

Commercial Code

DOCUMENTARY CREDITS

Article 720

The documentary credit is a credit issued by a bank upon request by the applicant for the benefit of a business partner of the applicant, and that is guaranteed by the possession of documents which represent the shipped goods or goods to be shipped, respectively.

The documentary credit is independent from the sales contract, which is the basis for the credit and from which the banks remain alien.

Article 721

The bank which issues the credit shall execute the provisions on payment, acceptance, discounting or negotiation provided for in the issuance of the credit on the condition that the documents comply with the conditions of the issued credit.

Article 722

The documentary credit can be revocable or irrevocable.
Unless otherwise expressly stipulated every credit is deemed irrevocable.

Article 723

The revocable credit does not bind the bank to the beneficiary. It may be modified or revoked by the bank at any moment either upon at the bank's own initiative or

---

[60] Bendjennet, *DCI*, vol. 1/3, p. 17, vol. 2/4, p. 23, on practical issues.

Tunisia

on the customer's request, and without duty to notify the beneficiary thereof, provided that the modification or revocation is neither effected in bad faith nor at an unreasonable time.

Article 724

The irrevocable credit creates a definite and direct undertaking by the bank to the beneficiary or the *bona fide* holder of issued drafts.

This undertaking may not be cancelled or modified without all involved parties' consent.

The irrevocable credit can be confirmed by another bank, which then assumes a definite and direct liability to the beneficiary.

The notification of the credit to the beneficiary by the involvement of another bank as such is not considered a confirmation of the credit by such bank.

Article 725

The bank shall assure that the documents strictly comply with the applicant's instructions.

If the bank refuses the documents it shall as soon as possible inform the applicant thereof and inform him of the detected discrepancies.

Article 726

The bank does not assume any responsibility if the documents on their face appear to comply with the received instructions.

The bank does not assume any responsibility regarding the goods which are subject to the issued credit.

Article 727

The documentary credit is not transferable or fractionable unless the bank which honours the credit for the beneficiary named by the applicant is authorized to make payment in whole or in part to several third parties upon instruction of the first beneficiary.

The credit is not transferable in the absence of express instructions by the issuing bank. Unless otherwise stipulated it may be transferred once only.

Turkey

General Remarks

Turkey is another country whose laws do not include specific provisions on documentary credits. It appears that documentary credits have not yet been subject to comprehensive academic research[61]. Turkish legal principles on documentary credits very much reflect Swiss law. However, they are strongly dominated by the UCP.

Unlike in Anglo-American law and in the UCP, a letter of credit in the meaning of Article 399 of the Law on Obligations is not regarded as a type of credit by Turkish law. Turkish law treats letters of credit as totally different from all other types of credits.

A choice of law for a documentary credit in principle is permitted. In the absence of such choice of law Turkish rules on conflict of laws subject the relationship between the issuing bank and the beneficiary to the laws of the place of performance[62].

---

[61] Özdamar, *Rechtsfragen des Dokumentenakkreditives in Gestalt seiner Regelung nach den ERA* (Revision 1983), 1996, with references to Turkish legal literature.
[62] See Özdamar, id., p. 187 et seq.

United Arab Emirates

General Remarks

The law on documentary credits is included in Articles 428 to 439 of the Commercial Code[63]. Supplement to Section on United Arab Emirates

Statutory provisions of the United Arab Emirates and the UCP treat certain issues identically, such as the distinction between revocable and irrevocable credits and the requirement of an expiry date of the credit which the United Arab Emirates' Commercial Code refers to as "validity date". However, the UCP are far more comprehensive.

The documentary credits statutes of the United Arab Emirates do not expressly state at which bank documents need to be presented prior to the credit's expiry date. This question was in dispute in case no. 136 of the Dubai Court of Appeals of 1999. In this case the beneficiary presented the documents prior to the expiry of the credit to the advising bank. This bank was nominated by the issuing bank to accept the documents; however, the credit did not provide for a place of presentation. By the time the documents were forwarded by the advising bank to the issuing bank the credit had expired and the issuing bank refused to honour the credit. The Court confirmed the issuing bank's opinion that documents must be presented to the issuing bank prior to the expiry date if the credit does not provide for a place of payment.

In case no. 395 of 1999 of the Abu Dhabi Court of Appeals an uncertainty about the effects of a waiver of discrepancies was clarified. The issue in dispute was whether a waiver of discrepancies by the applicant obligates or entitles the bank to accept discrepant documents. The Court stated that the bank no longer has a right to refuse to take up discrepant documents if the applicant waived the discrepancies. The bank then has no discretion whether or not to respect the waiver and is obligated to make payment to the beneficiary.

---

[63] Law No. 18/1993.

Commercial Code

Article 428 [Definition of a documentary credit]

1. The documentary credit is a contract according to which the bank issues a documentary credit for a specified amount and for a specified period of time upon a customer's (the person who asked for the credit) request in favour of a third person (the beneficiary), and which is guaranteed by documents that represent shipped goods or goods ready for shipment.

2. The documentary credit contract is independent from the contract for which the credit is issued and the bank remains alien to such contract.

Article 429 [Validity period]

Each documentary credit must specify a maximum validity date and the documents to be presented for payment, acceptance or discounting.

If the specified expiry date falls on a bank holiday the validity period shall be extended to the first working day following such bank holiday. Except for holidays the validity period shall not be extended even if the expiry date falls on a date on which the bank's business is interrupted due to *force majeure*, unless the credit's applicant gives express instructions to the contrary.

Article 430 [Relevant documents for credit opening]

1. The credit opening, confirmation or notification documents shall precisely define the documents against which payment, acceptance or discounting are to be made.

2. The issuing bank undertakes to carry out the conditions of payment, acceptance and discounting as stipulated by the credit, if documents that represent the goods comply with the terms and conditions of the credit.

Article 431 [Revocability of credit]

1. The documentary credit may be revocable or irrevocable.

2. The documentary credit shall be definite unless its revocability is expressly agreed upon.

3. The documentary credit may be fractionable, transferable, unfractionable or not transferable.

Article 432 [Irrevocable credit]

1. The irrevocable documentary credit does not create a liability by the bank towards the beneficiary and the bank may, at any time, modify or revoke such credit either at its own initiative or at the applicant's request.

United Arab Emirates

2. If the transport documents are presented in accordance with the terms and conditions of the documentary credit and within the stipulated period and prior to the credit's revocation, the bank and the applicant shall be jointly responsible to the beneficiary.

Article 433 [Bank's liability]

1. In the case of an irrevocable documentary credit, the bank's liability shall be definite and direct to the beneficiary and to any *bona fide* holder of the documents drawn in compliance with the contract for which the documentary credit has been issued.

2. The definite documentary credit may not be revoked or amended unless all involved parties agree.

Article 434 [Confirmation]

1. Any bank other than the one that issues the documentary credit may confirm the definite and irrevocable credit by fulfilling its commitment definitely and directly to the beneficiary and to any *bona fide* holder of the document in performing the credit opening contract.

2. The simple notification of the issuance of the definite documentary credit forwarded to the beneficiary by a bank other than the one that issues the documentary credit shall not be considered a confirmation of the credit by such bank.

Article 435 [Availability and Compliance of Documents]

1. The documents must be presented to the bank before the credit's expiry date. If they are presented after the expiry date the bank shall reject them unless the applicant accepts them and the bank agrees.

2. The bank shall assure that the documents are at its disposal, that they comply with the credit's conditions, and that they are in conformity with the credit.

Article 436 [Duty of examination]

The bank shall only be liable to examine the documents and to verify that they comply on their face with the documents stipulated in the credit. The bank shall not be liable for examining whether the goods themselves comply with the documents that represent them.

Article 437 [Transfer of documents]

The documents that are accepted by the bank shall be forwarded promptly to the applicant. If the bank rejects documents the bank shall notify the beneficiary promptly thereof and inform the beneficiary about the reasons for its rejection.

Article 438 [Transfer of Credit]

1. The beneficiary may not assign the credit in whole or in part to one or several third parties unless the beneficiary is authorized to do so by the bank and the credit expressly permits such transfer.

2. The bank may not pay the credit in parts unless the applicant authorizes the bank to do so.

3. The credit may be assigned only once unless otherwise provided for in the credit opening contract.

4. The assignment is effected either by endorsement of the credit if it is registered, or by actual transfer if the credit is for the benefit of its holder. If it is for a nominal amount it shall be remitted.

Article 439 [Parties' and bank's duties]

1. The applicant shall reimburse the bank for any amounts paid to the beneficiary according to the terms of the credit and compensate all expenses that have been incurred by the bank.

2. The bank shall be entitled to foreclose the documents that it received from the seller and to obtain a pledge over the goods that are represented by the documents as collateral for the bank's claims.

3. If the applicant fails to pay the bank the value of the transport documents that are in compliance with the credit within one month running from the date of the notification that such documents have been presented, the bank is entitled to sell the goods according to the provisions applicable to the execution of commercially pledged property.

4. If the goods have perished or been damaged the pledge shall apply to any amounts held in deposit.

5. After presentation of the documents the bank and its customer may agree that the customer transfers the goods that are subject to the credit in whole or in part to the bank as total or partial settlement of the customer's debt to the bank. The bank shall then authorize the customer to receive the goods and hold them in trust and sell them on behalf and for the account of the bank, at the terms and conditions agreed on between the parties. The customer shall be responsible as a commission agent and the bank shall have the rights of a trustee of the goods or their value.

United Arab Emirates

United Kingdom

General Remarks

The courts in the United Kingdom respect the international standards of documentary credit transactions. The principles of autonomy and strict compliance are acknowledged. Nevertheless, courts admit an interpretation of the language of a credit. Even if such interpretation turns out to be incorrect, banks may act in accordance with their understanding of the terms of the credit as long as the banks' interpretation of the credit is reasonable[64]. This view is consistent with the principle laid down in sub-Article 37 (c) of UCP 500 that "the description of the goods in the commercial invoice must correspond with the description in the Credit". The term "corresponding" does not require that identical words are used. This was confirmed in the Glencore case[65], where the court had to decide whether Indonesia (Inalum brand) in the invoice corresponded to the description, "any western brand", used in the credit. The London Commercial Court agreed with the bank that it was entitled to reject the invoice as not compliant while the Court of Appeal[66] found that the words of the invoice fell within the description of the invoice.

Fraud in the underlying trade transaction is regarded as a reason to prohibit the bank from honouring the credit. However, courts demand a certain level of evidence to demonstrate that the transaction was fraudulent. In general, affidavits by the plaintiff are regarded as one type of sufficient evidence[67]. If the bank honours the credit without being aware of discrepancies in the documents it may seek damages from the beneficiary if the beneficiary presents the documents with the knowledge that they are not compliant[68]. In the KBC Bank v. Industrials

---

[64] Crédit Agricole Indosuez v. Muslim Commercial Bank analyzed by Foster, *DCI*, vol. 6/4 p. 18.
[65] Jack, *DCI*, vol. 3/4 p. 10.
[66] Bayerische Vereinsbank/Glencore v. Bank of China, [1996] 1 Lloyd's Rep. 135.
[67] See Establishments Esefka International Anstalt v. Central Bank of Nigeria [1979] 1 Ll. Rep. 445.
[68] KBC Bank v. Industrial Steels (UK) Ltd, DC-PRO, 2000 Case Summaries.

Steels (UK) Ltd case the court regarded it as fraud if the beneficiary was aware of the discrepancies in the documents, made incorrect statements in presenting the documents and caused the bank to rely on those statements. No proof of dishonesty was required.

English courts and authors take the view that the applicable law of a credit is to be determined by the place of performance of the bank. This is not to be confused with the place of the bank's domicile. The place of performance is deemed to be the location at which the beneficiary shall present the documents in order to obtain payment and, thus, the applicable law is often determined to be the law of the confirming or paying bank.

The forum selection is treated more delicately by English courts. The domicile of the defendant is considered to be the general forum for a litigation. If the facts of a case show a great number of characteristics that link the case to a foreign jurisdiction, a court will refuse to hear the case owing to the existence of a more appropriate jurisdiction, provided that the defendant can present evidence that a more appropriate jurisdiction exists and that a trial in the United Kingdom is not more beneficial for the plaintiff than a trial in such other jurisdiction[69].

---

[69] <u>European Asian Bank AG v. Punjab & Sind Bank</u> [1981] 2 Ll. Rep. 651; for further issues, see Ridall, *DCI*, vol. 3/4 p. 19; Foster, *DCI* vol. 1/2 p. 21; *DCI*, vol. 2/2 p. 15; *DCI*, vol. 4/1 p. 21; *DCI*, vol. 4/3 p. 17.

United States of America

United States of America

General Remarks

Article 5 of the Uniform Commercial Code is the most comprehensive and detailed statutory coverage of documentary credits in the world. Although it addresses a wide range of practical and technical issues, it is considered to be incomplete (see UCC §5-102 (3)), and any issues not directly addressed by Article 5 need to be resolved by other provisions of law in the relevant US state and by legal principles.

Most provisions of Article 5 reflect case law prevailing at the time of the drafting of the provisions[70]. Surprisingly, the principle of strict compliance is not addressed by the statutory provisions. Nevertheless, US courts take a very narrow view with regard to non-conforming documents and adhere rigorously to the principle of strict compliance[71].

The law distinguishes between revocable and irrevocable credits. It does not, however, define whether a credit is revocable or irrevocable if the parties do not explicitly agree on this issue. UCC §5-116 permits the assignment of a credit if the credit is denominated transferable or assignable. Unlike the UCP, UCC §5-116 does not restrict the transferability of the credit to only one transfer. Regardless of the denomination of the credit as transferable or assignable the assignment of proceeds is expressly permitted.

---

[70] Käser, *Die gesetzliche Regelung des Akkreditivs und des Rembourses in den USA*, ZKW 1961, 1089.
[71] Mercado Agricola v. Mellon Bank International, 680 F.2d 43, 47 (2d Cir. 1979); Airlines Reporting Corp. v. Norwest Bank of Minnesota in *Annual Survey of Letter of Credit Law & Practice* 1996:414; Kredietbank Antwerp v. Midland Bank plc in *Annual Survey of Letter of Credit Law & Practice* 1998:450; Ocean Rig ASA v. Safra National Bank in *Annual Survey of Letter of Credit Law & Practice* 2000:345.

United States of America

the absence of specific language, a credit is considered to be revocable or irrevocable, Revised UCC §5-106(a) provides that a credit is only revocable if it so provides. Corresponding to the UCP, Revised UCC §5-112 and §5-114 distinguish between the transfer of the credit and the assignment of proceeds. While the assignment of proceeds can be effected by the beneficiary without the consent of the issuer or a nominated person, the transfer of the credit always requires that the credit be designated transferable. In addition, the time period during which a presentation shall be rejected or honoured has been adjusted to incorporate the seven-day period of Article 14 of UCP 500 (see Revised UCC §5-118(b)). Unlike UCP 500, however, Revised UCC Article 5 does not contain provisions concerning the transport documents referred to in UCP Articles 23 et seq., nor on tolerances in amounts and quantities.

Revised UCC Article 5 is more rigid with regard to the compliance of documents. Revised UCC §5-108(a) requires that an issuer shall honour a presentation that "appears on its face strictly to comply with the terms and conditions of the letter of credit". This reference to strict compliance, which was not included in the original UCC, reflects the history of court decisions, which, even prior to 1995, took a narrow view of the requirements regarding conformity of documents[2].

Revised UCC §5-116(c) reflects the previous acknowledgement of case law[3] that the UCP prevails if the parties agree on its application. However, the provisions of Revised UCC in UCC §5-103(c) cannot be modified; therefore they overrule any conflicting provisions in the UCP.

Revised UCC § 5-109 stipulates the requirements that need to be met to obtain injunctive relief in case of fraud, thereby providing more guidance to banks concerning their right to reject payment.

Typically, legislation on documentary credits does not contain rules on a statute of limitations or on judicial rules. These issues are governed by general national laws. By contrast, Revised UCC §5-115 and §5-116 contain special rules on the statute of limitations and the governing law for documentary credit transactions.

---

[2] Mercado Agricola v. Mellon Bank International, 680 F.2d 43, 47 (2d Cir. 1979); Airlines Reporting Corp. v. Norwest Bank of Minnesota in *Annual Survey of Letter of Credit Law & Practice* 1996:414; Kredietbank Antwerp v. Midland Bank plc in *Annual Survey of Letter of Credit Law & Practice* 1998:450; Ocean Rig ASA v. Safra National Bank in *Annual Survey of Letter of Credit Law & Practice* 2000:345.

[3] Valenstein/Hartley, *DCI*, vol. 1/3, p.18 with reference to Banca Del Sempione v. Suriel Finance NV and Provident Bank of Maryland, 842 F.Supp. 417 (Md. 1994).

ERRATA

Documentary Credit Law throughout the world (ICC publication No. 633)

Pages 120–121

The "General Remarks" section of the chapter on the United States of America in the original text applied to the version of Article 5 of the Uniform Commercial Code (UCC) that was in force before a Revision was adopted in 1995. The following text more closely parallels the situation in place in the United States as of this writing, and it should be used in place of the General Remarks in the original text.

United States of America

General Remarks

In 1952 a model law on letters of credit was introduced as Article 5 of the Uniform Commercial Code ("UCC"). In the subsequent years this model law was adopted by all US states. It was not until 1995 that a revision of Article 5 of the UCC ("Revised Article 5 ") was adopted, which, as of this writing, has been enacted in all US states with the exception of Georgia and Wisconsin. The latter anticipates that it will implement Revised UCC Article 5 in 2002.

Revised UCC Article 5 aims to bring the legislation on letters of credit up-to-date with new standards in technology and to reflect the interpretation of the original UCC Article 5 by the courts[1].

Like the original, Revised UCC Article 5 is the most comprehensive and detailed statutory coverage of documentary credits worldwide. Although it no longer contains an explicit acknowledgment that it is an incomplete set of rules, as previously stated in UCC §5-112(3), it is still not an all-embracing statute. Any issues not directly addressed by Revised UCC Article 5 are governed by the applicable written law and case law.

Revised UCC Article 5 more closely follows the UCP than did its predecessor statute. While Article 5 of the UCC remains silent on the question of whether, in

---

[1] Allen/Pollack, *Letters of Credit – An Under Estimated Finance Vehicle*, Festschrift für Martin Pelzer, 2001, p. 5

Unlike many civil law jurisdictions, US courts are rather generous in granting motions for injunctive relief against banks that do not perform under a credit. Based on the wording of UCC §5-114 (2), fraud, forgery or any kind of similar misconduct obligates the bank to refuse to honour a credit irrespective of whether such misconduct or fraud stems from the relationship between the beneficiary and the bank or the beneficiary and the applicant[72].

It is acknowledged that the UCP prevails if the parties agree on its application[73]. Thus, the provisions of Article 5 of the UCC in practice provide for fall-back rules if the parties subject a credit to the application of the UCP and the UCP do not address an issue in dispute[74].

Uniform Commercial Code

Article V [Letters of Credit]

§5-101 – Short title

This article may be cited as Uniform Commercial Code – Letters of Credit.

§ 5-102 – Definitions

a) In this article:

   1. *"Adviser"* means a person who, at the request of the issuer, a confirmer, or another adviser, notifies or requests another adviser to notify the beneficiary that a letter of credit has been issued, confirmed, or amended.

   2. *"Applicant"* means a person at whose request or for whose account a letter of credit is issued. The term includes a person who requests an issuer to issue a letter of credit on behalf of another if the person making the request undertakes an obligation to reimburse the issuer.

---

[72] Itek Corp. v. First National Bank, 730 F. 2d 19 (1st. Cir. 1984); Emery-Waterhouse Company v. Rhode Island National Hospital Trust National Bank, 757 F. 2d 399 (1st Cir. 1985); Penn State Construction v. Cambria Savings & Loan Association, 519 F. 2d 1034 (Penn. 1987); Regent Corp. v. Azmat Bangladesh in *Annual Survey of Letter of Credit Law & Practice* 1998:486; see also Shingleton/Wilmer, *Einstweiliger Rechtsschutz im internationalen Dokumentenakkreditivgeschäft nach deutschem und amerikanischen Recht*, RIW 1991, 793.

[73] Valenstein/Hartley, *DCI*, vol. 1/3, p.18 with reference to Banca Del Sempione v. Suriel Finance NV and Provident Bank of Maryland, 842 F.Supp. 417 (Md. 1994).

[74] Valenstein *DCI*, vol. 1/1, p. 22 with reference to Alaska Textile Co., Inc. Chase Manhattan Bank, 982, F. 2d 813, 816 (2d Cir. 1992).

United States of America

3. *"Beneficiary"* means a person who under the terms of a letter of credit is entitled to have its complying presentation honored. The term includes a person to whom drawing rights have been transferred under a transferable letter of credit.

4. *"Confirmer"* means a nominated person who undertakes, at the request or with the consent of the issuer, to honor a presentation under a letter of credit issued by another.

5. *"Dishonor"* of a letter of credit means failure timely to honor or to take an interim action, such as acceptance of a draft, that may be required by the letter of credit.

6. *"Document"* means a draft or other demand, document of title, investment security, certificate, invoice, or other record, statement, or representation of fact, law, right, or opinion (i) which is presented in a written or other medium permitted by the letter of credit or, unless prohibited by the letter of credit, by the standard practice referred to in Section 5-108(e) and (ii) which is capable of being examined for compliance with the terms and conditions of the letter of credit. A document may not be oral.

7. *"Good faith"* means honesty in fact in the conduct or transaction concerned.

8. *"Honor"* of a letter of credit means performance of the issuer's undertaking in the letter of credit to pay or deliver an item of value. Unless the letter of credit otherwise provides, "honor" occurs
   (i) upon payment,
   (ii) if the letter of credit provides for acceptance, upon acceptance of a draft and, at maturity, its payment, or
   (iii) if the letter of credit provides for incurring a deferred obligation, upon incurring the obligation and, at maturity, its performance.

9. *"Issuer"* means a bank or other person that issues a letter of credit, but does not include an individual who makes an engagement for personal, family, or household purposes.

10. *"Letter of credit"* means a definite undertaking that satisfies the requirements of Section 5-104 by an issuer to a beneficiary at the request or for the account of an applicant or, in the case of a financial institution, to itself or for its own account, to honor a documentary presentation by payment or delivery of an item of value.

11. *"Nominated person"* means a person whom the issuer (i) designates or authorizes to pay, accept, negotiate, or otherwise give value under a letter of credit and (ii) undertakes by agreement or custom and practice to reimburse.

12. *"Presentation"* means delivery of a document to an issuer or nominated person for honor or giving of value under a letter of credit.

13. *"Presenter"* means a person making a presentation as or on behalf of a beneficiary or nominated person.

14. *"Record"* means information that is inscribed on a tangible medium, or that is stored in an electronic or other medium and is retrievable in perceivable form.

15. *"Successor of a beneficiary"* means a person who succeeds to substantially all of the rights of a beneficiary by operation of law, including a corporation with or into which the beneficiary has been merged or consolidated, an administrator, executor, personal representative, trustee in bankruptcy, debtor in possession, liquidator, and receiver.

b) Definitions in other Articles applying to this article and the sections in which they appear are:

"Accept" or "Acceptance"	Section 3-409
"Value"	Sections 3-303, 4-211

c) Article 1 contains additional general definitions and principles.

§5-103 – Scope

a) This article applies to letters of credit and to certain rights and obligations arising out of transactions involving letters of credit.

b) The statement of a rule in this article does not by itself require, imply, or negate application of the same or a different rule to a situation not provided for, or to a person not specified, in this article.

c) With the exception of this subsection, subsections (a) and (d), Sections 5-102(a)(9) and (10), 5-106(d), and 5-114(d), and except to the extent prohibited in Sections 1-102(3) and 5-117(d), the effect of this article may be varied by agreement or by a provision stated or incorporated by reference in an undertaking. A term in an agreement or undertaking generally excusing liability or generally limiting remedies for failure to perform obligations is not sufficient to vary obligations prescribed by this article.

d) Rights and obligations of an issuer to a beneficiary or a nominated person under a letter of credit are independent of the existence, performance, or nonperformance of a contract or arrangement out of which the letter of credit arises or which underlies it, including contracts or arrangements between the issuer and the applicant and between the applicant and the beneficiary.

United States of America

§5-104 – Formal requirements

A letter of credit, confirmation, advice, transfer, amendment, or cancellation may be issued in any form that is a record and is authenticated (i) by a signature or (ii) in accordance with the agreement of the parties or the standard practice referred to in Section 5-108(e).

§5-105 – Consideration

Consideration is not required to issue, amend, transfer, or cancel a letter of credit, advice, or confirmation.

§5-106 – Issuance, amendment, cancellation, and duration

a) A letter of credit is issued and becomes enforceable according to its terms against the issuer when the issuer sends or otherwise transmits it to the person requested to advise or to the beneficiary. A letter of credit is revocable only if it so provides.

b) After a letter of credit is issued, rights and obligations of a beneficiary, applicant, confirmer, and issuer are not affected by an amendment or cancellation to which that person has not consented except to the extent the letter of credit provides that it is revocable or that the issuer may amend or cancel the letter of credit without that consent.

c) If there is no stated expiration date or other provision that determines its duration, a letter of credit expires one year after its stated date of issuance or, if none is stated, after the date on which it is issued.

d) A letter of credit that states that it is perpetual expires five years after its stated date of issuance, or if none is stated, after the date on which it is issued.

§5-107 – Confirmer, nominated person, and adviser

a) A confirmer is directly obligated on a letter of credit and has the rights and obligations of an issuer to the extent of its confirmation. The confirmer also has rights against and obligations to the issuer as if the issuer were an applicant and the confirmer had issued the letter of credit at the request and for the account of the issuer.

b) A nominated person who is not a confirmer is not obligated to honor or otherwise give value for a presentation.

c) A person requested to advise may decline to act as an adviser. An adviser that is not a confirmer is not obligated to honor or give value for a presentation.

An adviser undertakes to the issuer and to the beneficiary accurately to advise the terms of the letter of credit, confirmation, amendment, or advice received by that person and undertakes to the beneficiary to check the apparent authenticity of the request to advise. Even if the advice is inaccurate, the letter of credit, confirmation, or amendment is enforceable as issued.

d) A person who notifies a transferee beneficiary of the terms of a letter of credit, confirmation, amendment, or advice has the rights and obligations of an adviser under subsection (c). The terms in the notice to the transferee beneficiary may differ from the terms in any notice to the transferor beneficiary to the extent permitted by the letter of credit, confirmation, amendment, or advice received by the person who so notifies.

§5-108 – Issuer's rights and obligations

a) Except as otherwise provided in Section 5-109, an issuer shall honor a presentation that, as determined by the standard practice referred to in subsection (e), appears on its face strictly to comply with the terms and conditions of the letter of credit. Except as otherwise provided in Section 5-113 and unless otherwise agreed with the applicant, an issuer shall dishonor a presentation that does not appear so to comply.

b) An issuer has a reasonable time after presentation, but not beyond the end of the seventh business day of the issuer after the day of its receipt of documents:
   1. to honor,
   2. if the letter of credit provides for honor to be completed more than seven business days after presentation, to accept a draft or incur a deferred obligation, or
   3. to give notice to the presenter of discrepancies in the presentation.

c) Except as otherwise provided in subsection (d), an issuer is precluded from asserting as a basis for dishonor any discrepancy if timely notice is not given, or any discrepancy not stated in the notice if timely notice is given.

d) Failure to give the notice specified in subsection (b) or to mention fraud, forgery, or expiration in the notice does not preclude the issuer from asserting as a basis for dishonor fraud or forgery as described in Section 5-109(a) or expiration of the letter of credit before presentation.

e) An issuer shall observe standard practice of financial institutions that regularly issue letters of credit. Determination of the issuer's observance of the standard practice is a matter of interpretation for the court. The court shall offer the parties a reasonable opportunity to present evidence of the standard practice.

f) An issuer is not responsible for:
    1. the performance or nonperformance of the underlying contract, arrangement, or transaction,
    2. an act or omission of others, or
    3. observance or knowledge of the usage of a particular trade other than the standard practice referred to in subsection (e).

g) If an undertaking constituting a letter of credit under Section 5-102(a)(10) contains nondocumentary conditions, an issuer shall disregard the nondocumentary conditions and treat them as if they were not stated.

h) An issuer that has dishonored a presentation shall return the documents or hold them at the disposal of, and send advice to that effect to, the presenter.

i) An issuer that has honored a presentation as permitted or required by this article:
    1. is entitled to be reimbursed by the applicant in immediately available funds not later than the date of its payment of funds;
    2. takes the documents free of claims of the beneficiary or presenter;
    3. is precluded from asserting a right of recourse on a draft under Sections 3-414 and 3-415;
    4. except as otherwise provided in Sections 5-110 and 5-117, is precluded from restitution of money paid or other value given by mistake to the extent the mistake concerns discrepancies in the documents or tender which are apparent on the face of the presentation; and
    5. is discharged to the extent of its performance under the letter of credit unless the issuer honored a presentation in which a required signature of a beneficiary was forged.

§5-109 – Fraud and forgery

a) If a presentation is made that appears on its face strictly to comply with the terms and conditions of the letter of credit, but a required document is forged or materially fraudulent, or honor of the presentation would facilitate a material fraud by the beneficiary on the issuer or applicant:
    1. the issuer shall honor the presentation, if honor is demanded by (i) a nominated person who has given value in good faith and without notice of forgery or material fraud, (ii) a confirmer who has honored its confirmation in good faith, (iii) a holder in due course of a draft drawn under the letter of credit which was taken after acceptance by the issuer or nominated person, or (iv) an assignee of the issuer's or nominated person's deferred obligation that was taken for value and without notice of forgery or material fraud after the obligation was incurred by the issuer or nominated person; and

2. the issuer, acting in good faith, may honor or dishonor the presentation in any other case.

b) If an applicant claims that a required document is forged or materially fraudulent or that honor of the presentation would facilitate a material fraud by the beneficiary on the issuer or applicant, a court of competent jurisdiction may temporarily or permanently enjoin the issuer from honoring a presentation or grant similar relief against the issuer or other persons only if the court finds that:
    1. the relief is not prohibited under the law applicable to an accepted draft or deferred obligation incurred by the issuer;
    2. a beneficiary, issuer, or nominated person who may be adversely affected is adequately protected against loss that it may suffer because the relief is granted;
    3. all of the conditions to entitle a person to the relief under the law of this State have been met; and
    4. on the basis of the information submitted to the court, the applicant is more likely than not to succeed under its claim of forgery or material fraud and the person demanding honor does not qualify for protection under subsection (a)(1).

§5-110 – *Warranties*

a) If its presentation is honored, the beneficiary warrants:
    1. to the issuer, any other person to whom presentation is made, and the applicant that there is no fraud or forgery of the kind described in Section 5-109(a); and
    2. to the applicant that the drawing does not violate any agreement between the applicant and beneficiary or any other agreement intended by them to be augmented by the letter of credit.

b) The warranties in subsection (a) are in addition to warranties arising under Article 3, 4, 7, and 8 because of the presentation or transfer of documents covered by any of those articles.

§5-111 – *Remedies*

a) If an issuer wrongfully dishonors or repudiates its obligation to pay money under a letter of credit before presentation, the beneficiary, successor, or nominated person presenting on its own behalf may recover from the issuer the amount that is the subject of the dishonor or repudiation. If the issuer's obligation under the letter of credit is not for the payment of money, the

United States of America

claimant may obtain specific performance or, at the claimant's election, recover an amount equal to the value of performance from the issuer. In either case, the claimant may also recover incidental but not consequential damages. The claimant is not obligated to take action to avoid damages that might be due from the issuer under this subsection. If, although not obligated to do so, the claimant avoids damages, the claimant's recovery from the issuer must be reduced by the amount of damages avoided. The issuer has the burden of proving the amount of damages avoided. In the case of repudiation the claimant need not present any document.

b) If an issuer wrongfully dishonors a draft or demand presented under a letter of credit or honors a draft or demand in breach of its obligation to the applicant, the applicant may recover damages resulting from the breach, including incidental but not consequential damages, less any amount saved as a result of the breach.

c) If an adviser or nominated person other than a confirmer breaches an obligation under this article or an issuer breaches an obligation not covered in subsection (a) or (b), a person to whom the obligation is owed may recover damages resulting from the breach, including incidental but not consequential damages, less any amount saved as a result of the breach. To the extent of the confirmation, a confirmer has the liability of an issuer specified in this subsection and subsections (a) and (b).

d) An issuer, nominated person, or adviser who is found liable under subsection (a), (b), or (c) shall pay interest on the amount owed thereunder from the date of wrongful dishonor or other appropriate date.

e) Reasonable attorney's fees and other expenses of litigation must be awarded to the prevailing party in an action in which a remedy is sought under this article.

f) Damages that would otherwise be payable by a party for breach of an obligation under this article may be liquidated by agreement or undertaking, but only in an amount or by a formula that is reasonable in light of the harm anticipated.

§5-112 – Transfer of letter of credit

a) Except as otherwise provided in Section 5-113, unless a letter of credit provides that it is transferable, the right of a beneficiary to draw or otherwise demand performance under a letter of credit may not be transferred.

b) Even if a letter of credit provides that it is transferable, the issuer may refuse to recognize or carry out a transfer if:

1. the transfer would violate applicable law; or

2. the transferor or transferee has failed to comply with any requirement stated in the letter of credit or any other requirement relating to transfer imposed by the issuer which is within the standard practice referred to in Section 5-108(e) or is otherwise reasonable under the circumstances.

§5-113 – Transfer by operation of law

a) A successor of a beneficiary may consent to amendments, sign and present documents, and receive payment or other items of value in the name of the beneficiary without disclosing its status as a successor.

b) A successor of a beneficiary may consent to amendments, sign and present documents, and receive payment or other items of value in its own name as the disclosed successor of the beneficiary. Except as otherwise provided in subsection (e), an issuer shall recognize a disclosed successor of a beneficiary as beneficiary in full substitution for its predecessor upon compliance with the requirements for recognition by the issuer of a transfer of drawing rights by operation of law under the standard practice referred to in Section 5-108(e) or, in the absence of such a practice, compliance with other reasonable procedures sufficient to protect the issuer.

c) An issuer is not obliged to determine whether a purported successor is a successor of a beneficiary or whether the signature of a purported successor is genuine or authorized.

d) Honor of a purported successor's apparently complying presentation under subsection (a) or (b) has the consequences specified in Section 5-108(i) even if the purported successor is not the successor of a beneficiary. Documents signed in the name of the beneficiary or of a disclosed successor by a person who is neither the beneficiary nor the successor of the beneficiary are forged documents for the purposes of Section 5-109.

e) An issuer whose rights of reimbursement are not covered by subsection (d) or substantially similar law and any confirmer or nominated person may decline to recognize a presentation under subsection (b).

f) A beneficiary whose name is changed after the issuance of a letter of credit has the same rights and obligations as a successor of a beneficiary under this section.

§5-114 – Assignment of proceeds

a) In this section, *"proceeds of a letter of credit"* means the cash, check, accepted draft, or other item of value paid or delivered upon honor or giving of value by the issuer or any nominated person under the letter of credit. The term does not include a beneficiary's drawing rights or documents presented by the beneficiary.

United States of America

b) A beneficiary may assign its right to part or all of the proceeds of a letter of credit. The beneficiary may do so before presentation as a present assignment of its right to receive proceeds contingent upon its compliance with the terms and conditions of the letter of credit.

c) An issuer or nominated person need not recognize an assignment of proceeds of a letter of credit until it consents to the assignment.

d) An issuer or nominated person has no obligation to give or withhold its consent to an assignment of proceeds of a letter of credit, but consent may not be unreasonably withheld if the assignee possesses and exhibits the letter of credit and presentation of the letter of credit is a condition to honor.

e) Rights of a transferee beneficiary or nominated person are independent of the beneficiary's assignment of the proceeds of a letter of credit and are superior to the assignee's right to the proceeds.

f) Neither the rights recognized by this section between an assignee and an issuer, transferee beneficiary, or nominated person nor the issuer's or nominated person's payment of proceeds to an assignee or a third person affect the rights between the assignee and any person other than the issuer, transferee beneficiary, or nominated person. The mode of creating and perfecting a security interest in or granting an assignment of a beneficiary's rights to proceeds is governed by Article 9 or other law. Against persons other than the issuer, transferee beneficiary, or nominated person, the rights and obligations arising upon the creation of a security interest or other assignment of a beneficiary's right to proceeds and its perfection are governed by Article 9 or other law.

§5-115 – Statute of limitations

An action to enforce a right or obligation arising under this article must be commenced within one year after the expiration date of the relevant letter of credit or one year after the [claim for relief] [cause of action] accrues, whichever occurs later. A [claim for relief] [cause of action] accrues when the breach occurs, regardless of the aggrieved party's lack of knowledge of the breach.

§5-116 – Choice of law and forum

a) The liability of an issuer, nominated person, or adviser for action or omission is governed by the law of the jurisdiction chosen by an agreement in the form of a record signed or otherwise authenticated by the affected parties in the manner provided in Section 5-104 or by a provision in the person's letter of credit, confirmation, or other undertaking. The jurisdiction whose law is chosen need not bear any relation to the transaction.

b) Unless subsection (a) applies, the liability of an issuer, nominated person, or adviser for action or omission is governed by the law of the jurisdiction in which the person is located. The person is considered to be located at the address indicated in the person's undertaking. If more than one address is indicated, the person is considered to be located at the address from which the person's undertaking was issued. For the purpose of jurisdiction, choice of law, and recognition of interbranch letters of credit, but not enforcement of a judgment, all branches of a bank are considered separate juridical entities and a bank is considered to be located at the place where its relevant branch is considered to be located under this subsection.

c) Except as otherwise provided in this subsection, the liability of an issuer, nominated person, or adviser is governed by any rules of custom or practice, such as the Uniform Customs and Practice for Documentary Credits, to which the letter of credit, confirmation, or other undertaking is expressly made subject. If (i) this article would govern the liability of an issuer, nominated person, or adviser under subsection (a) or (b), (ii) the relevant undertaking incorporates rules of custom or practice, and (iii) there is conflict between this article and those rules as applied to that undertaking, those rules govern except to the extent of any conflict with the nonvariable provisions specified in Section 5-103(c).

d) If there is conflict between this article and Article 3, 4, 4A, or 9, this article governs.

e) The forum for settling disputes arising out of an undertaking within this article may be chosen in the manner and with the binding effect that governing law may be chosen in accordance with subsection (a).

§5-117 – Subrogation of issuer, applicant, and nominated person

a) An issuer that honors a beneficiary's presentation is subrogated to the rights of the beneficiary to the same extent as if the issuer were a secondary obligor of the underlying obligation owed to the beneficiary and of the applicant to the same extent as if the issuer were the secondary obligor of the underlying obligation owed to the applicant.

b) An applicant that reimburses an issuer is subrogated to the rights of the issuer against any beneficiary, presenter, or nominated person to the same extent as if the applicant were the secondary obligor of the obligations owed to the issuer and has the rights of subrogation of the issuer to the rights of the beneficiary stated in subsection (a).

United States of America

United States of America

c) A nominated person who pays or gives value against a draft or demand presented under a letter of credit is subrogated to the rights of:

1. the issuer against the applicant to the same extent as if the nominated person were a secondary obligor of the obligation owed to the issuer by the applicant;

2. the beneficiary to the same extent as if the nominated person were a secondary obligor of the underlying obligation owed to the beneficiary; and

3. the applicant to same extent as if the nominated person were a secondary obligor of the underlying obligation owed to the applicant.

d) Notwithstanding any agreement or term to the contrary, the rights of subrogation stated in subsections (a) and (b) do not arise until the issuer honors the letter of credit or otherwise pays and the rights in subsection (c) do not arise until the nominated person pays or otherwise gives value. Until then, the issuer, nominated person, and the applicant do not derive under this section present or prospective rights forming the basis of a claim, defense, or excuse.

Yemen

General Remarks

Until their unification in 1990, the two Yemeni states applied different sets of laws on documentary credits[75]. The present-day law on documentary credits is harmonized and incorporated in Articles 400 to 407 of the Commercial Code[76]. Yemen has implemented the provisions of the Kuwaiti law.

Commercial Code

Article 400

1. The documentary credit is an agreement by which the bank undertakes to issue a credit upon a customer's (the applicant) request for the benefit of a third party (the beneficiary) which is guaranteed by documents that represent transported goods or goods ready for transport.

2. The documentary credit shall be independent from the contract for which it is issued. The bank shall remain alien to such contract.

Article 401

The documents against which payments, acceptance or discounting are to be made shall be specified in the request to issue the documentary credit, its confirmation or notification.

Article 402

If the documents comply with the terms and conditions of the documentary credit, the issuing bank shall effect payment, acceptance or discounting as provided for in the credit.

---

[75] See Schütze, *Das Dokumentenakkreditiv im internationalen Handelsverkehr*, 5th ed. 1999, p. 606.
[76] Law No. 32/1991.

Yemen

Article 403

1. The documentary credit may be confirmed or revocable.

2. The credit opening contract shall define expressly the type of the credit. In the absence of such express definition the credit shall be deemed revocable.

Article 404

The revocable credit does not create an obligation of the bank to the beneficiary. The bank may modify or cancel the credit at all times either at its own initiative or the applicant's request without being required to notify the beneficiary, provided that the modification or cancellation is done in good faith and in a reasonable time.

Article 405

1. By an irrevocable credit the bank undertakes a direct and definite obligation to the beneficiary or any good faith holder of the documents specified in the application to issue the credit.

2. An irrevocable documentary credit may not be cancelled or modified unless all concerned parties agree.

3. An irrevocable credit may be confirmed by another bank which then undertakes a direct and definite obligation to the beneficiary.

4. The simple notification of opening a documentary credit forwarded to the beneficiary via another bank shall not be deemed a confirmation of the credit.

Article 406

1. An irrevocable documentary credit shall contain an expiry date for its validity by which the documents need to be presented to effect payment, acceptance or discounting.

2. If the expiry date of the credit's validity falls on a bank holiday the validity period shall be extended to the first working day following the bank holiday.

3. Except for bank holidays, the credit's validity shall not be extended even if the expiry date falls in a period during which the bank's business is interrupted by *force majeure*, unless the applicant expressly agrees to an extension.

Article 407

1. The bank shall examine whether the documents comply with the instructions of the applicant of the credit.

2. If the bank refuses the documents it shall immediately notify the beneficiary by specifying the reasons for refusal.

Article 408

1. The bank does not assume any liability if the presented documents on their face appear to comply with the applicant's instructions.

2. The bank shall not be liable for the performance of consignors and insurers of the goods for which payment the credit has been issued, their quality, weight, condition, packaging or value.

Article 409

The documentary credit may not be assigned in part or in whole unless the issuing bank is authorized by the applicant to make payment on the credit in accordance with the applicant's instructions in part or in full to one or several third parties. The credit may not be assigned unless the concerned bank agrees to the assignment. The credit may be assigned only once unless otherwise agreed upon.

Article 410

If the applicant does not pay the bank the value of the consignment documents according to the terms of the credit within three months running from the date on which the applicant is notified that the documents have been presented, the bank may sell the goods in accordance with the execution proceedings applicable to commercially pledged property.

Yemen

Yugoslavia

General Remarks

§§ 1072 to 1082 of the Law on Contracts govern documentary credits. These provisions were also implemented in the laws of other states which previously belonged to Yugoslavia. Under Yugoslavian law documentary credits in general are deemed revocable.

Law on Contracts

Liabilities of the issuing bank and form of the credit – §1072

1. By accepting the applicant's request to issue a letter of credit the issuing bank undertakes to pay the addressee a certain amount of money if the conditions as included in the request to issue a credit are met within a certain time.

2. The credit must be in writing.

When does the liability to the addressee arise? – §1073

1. The bank shall be liable to the addressee from the day on which the issuance of the credit has been notified to the addressee.

2. The applicant shall be bound to the request from the time at which this request was received by the bank.

Independence of the credit from any other transactions – §1074

The credit is independent from the sales agreement or any other transaction for which the credit has been issued.

Documentary credit – §1075

A documentary credit exists if the bank undertakes to pay the credit's addressee a certain amount of money, provided that documents are presented according to the conditions set forth in the credit.

Yugoslavia

Undertaking of the issuing bank – §1076

The bank which issues the documentary credit undertakes to comply with the payment clauses according to the conditions as provided by the credit.

Types of credit – §1077

1. The documentary credit can be revocable or irrevocable.

2. Unless expressly agreed otherwise the credit is always revocable also if it is issued for a certain period of time.

Revocable credit – §1078

The revocable credit does not bind the bank to the addressee. For this reason the bank may at any time upon the applicant's request or on its own initiative exchange the credit or revoke it if this is in the applicant's interest.

Irrevocable credit – §1079

1. The irrevocable documentary credit is an independent and direct undertaking by the bank to the credit's addressee.

2. Such undertaking can only be cancelled or amended by agreement of all involved parties.

3. The irrevocable documentary credit may be confirmed by another bank which thereby assumes an independent and direct liability to the addressee.

4. The notification of the credit by another bank as such is not a confirmation of the credit.

Duties of the bank regarding documents – §1080

1. The bank is obliged to examine whether the documents fully comply with the applicant's demands.

2. The bank must within the shortest possible time after receipt of the documents inform the applicant about their receipt and any irregularities and insufficiencies.

Limits of the bank's liability – §1081

1. The bank does not assume any liability if the presented documents on their face appear to comply with the instructions by the applicant.

Yugoslavia

2. The bank does not assume any liability with regard to the goods which are subject to the issued credit.

Transferability and fractionability of the credit – §1082

1. The documentary credit can only be transferred or fractioned if the bank that issued the credit for the benefit of the addressee as denominated by the applicant is authorized by the instruction of the first addressee to make payment in full or in part to one or a greater number of third parties.

2. The credit may be transferred only by the issuing bank and only once upon express instructions unless otherwise agreed.

The following countries are not known to have specific rules on documentary credits

Algeria	Iran	Puerto Rico
Antigua	Jamaica	Romania
Argentina	Japan	Saudi Arabia
Aruba	Kenya	Slovenia
Australia	Kiribati	Solomon Islands
Azores	Luxembourg	South Africa
Bahamas	Madeira	Spain[90]
Bangladesh[77]	Mali	Sri Lanka[91]
Barbados	Malta[86]	St Kitts
Belgium[78]	Montserrat	Korea
Cayman Islands	Morocco	St Lucia
Channel Islands	Namibia	St Vincent
China[79]	Netherlands[87]	Senegal
Cook Islands	Netherlands Antilles	Surinam
Costa Rica	New Caledonia	Sweden[92]
Croatia	New Zealand	Taiwan
Cyprus[80]	Nicaragua	Tonga
Denmark[81]	Nieu Island	Trinidad and Tobago
Dominican Republic	Nigeria	Tuvalu
Ecuador	Norway[88]	Uganda
Fiji	Pakistan	Ukraine
Finland[82]	Panama	Uruguay
France[83]	Papua New Guinea	Vanuatu
Ghana	Paraguay	Venezuela
Gibraltar	Peru	Vietnam[93]
Iceland[84]	Philippines	Western Samoa
India[85]	Poland[89]	Zaire
Indonesia	Portugal	Zimbabwe

NOTES

[77] Regarding some practical issues, see Babar, *DCI*, vol. 6/4 p. 16.

[78] For reports on Belgian documentary credit practice, see Puelinckx, *DCI*, vol. 1/1 p. 18; Franck, *DCI* , vol. 3/1 p. 18, which highlights difficulties arising from the common absence of jurisdiction and choice of law agreements.

[79] For practice reports see Wie Liaju, *DCI*, vol. 1/2, p. 19; Jian, *DCI*, vol. 2/1 p. 15; *DCI*, vol. 2/4 p. 21; *DCI*, vol. 3/2 p. 17; *DCI*, vol. 4/1 p. 20; *DCI*, vol. 4/3 (on back-to-back LC); *DCI*, vol. 5/2 p. 19; *DCI*, vol. 6/4 p. 17.

[80] For practice reports see, Theodorou, *DCI*, vol. 1/1 p.19; vol. 1/4 p. 16; vol. 2/3 p. 17; vol. 2/4 p. 22; vol. 3/4 p. 18; vol. 4/2 p. 21.

[81] Langerich, *DCI*, vol. 1/4 p. 17; Engelholm, *DCI* vol. 1/1 p.20; Engelholm/Malqvist, *DCI* vol. 3/2 p. 18; vol. 4/1 p. 20; Malmqvist, *DCI* vol. 5/1 p. 13.

[82] See Heino, *DCI*, vol. 1/2 p. 19, for practical information.

[83] Boudinot, *Pratique du crédit documentaire*, 1979; Eisemann/Bontoux/Rowe, *Le crédit documentaire dans le commerce extérieur*, 1985; for further references, see Schütze, *Das Dokumentenakkreditiv im internationalen Handelsverkehr*, 5th ed. 1999, p. 361; on French practice: BNP, *DCI*, vol. 2/2 p. 14, reporting on two interesting court cases.

[84] See the practice reports by Magnússon, *DCI*, vol. 1/11 p.20; Júllusdóttir, *DCI*, vol. 2/2 p. 14.

[85] For practical questions, see Ravi Mehta, *DCI*, vol. 5/2 p. 20; *DCI*, vol. 6/1 p. 17; *DCI*, vol. 6/3 p. 18, reporting on the interesting "competition" between documentary credits and export insurance.

[86] For a practice report, see Gauchi, *DCI*, vol. 1/4 p. 18.

[87] For a practice report, see Scholtz, *DCI*, vol. 1/1 p. 21.

[88] For a report on Norwegian practice, see Siebke, *DCI*, vol. 1/3 p. 16

[89] See Skawinska-Lijk, *DCI*, vol. 1/3 p. 16; Werwinska, *DCI*, vol. 3/1 p. 19, on certain practical questions.

[90] See Claveria, *DCI*, vol. 3/2 p. 19, which reports on an interesting Catalonian alternative to documentary credits.

[91] See the practice report by Peiris, *DCI*, vol. 2/2 p. 16.

[92] For information on Swedish documentary credits practice, see Ostwald, *DCI*, vol. 1/1 p. 21.

[93] For information on the practice, see Le Minh Tam, *DCI*, vol. 2/1 p. 18; *DCI*, vol. 2/3 p. 19.

Annexes

- BIBLIOGRAPHY
- ICC UNIFORM CUSTOMS AND PRACTICE FOR DOCUMENTARY CREDITS (UCP 500)
- ICC AT A GLANCE
- SELECTED ICC PUBLICATIONS

Selected Literature on Documentary Credits[1]

Angersbach

Beiträge zum Institut des Dokumenten-Akkreditivs, Diss. Würzburg 1965

Avancini/Iro/Koziol

Österreichisches Bankvertragsrecht, vol. II, 1993, p. 357 et seq.

Balossini

'Il credito documentario nelle teorie prevalente e nell'ultima revisione delle corme ed usi uniformi', in: Portale, *Le operazione bancarie*, vol. II, 1978, p. 981 et seq.

Balossini

Norme ed Usi Uniformi relativi ai Crediti Documentari, 4th ed.,1988

Begin

Le crédit documentaire irrévocable utilisé à titre d'instrument de paiement en droit civil québecois, thèse McGill 1985

Bisset

A Guide to Documentary Credit and Collections, 1981

Borggrefe

Akkreditiv und Grundverhältnis, 1971

Boudinot

Pratique du crédit documentaire, 1979

del Busto

ICC Guide to Documentary Credit Operations, ICC publication No. 515, 1993

del Busto

Case Studies on Documentary Credits under UCP 500, ICC publication No. 535, 1995

Canaris

Bankvertragsrecht, 4th ed., 1988, Notes 916 et seq.

Caprioli

Le crédit documentaire: évolution et perspectives, 1992

Davis

The Documentary Credit Handbook, 1988

Dekker

Case Studies on Documentary Credits, ICC publication No. 459, 1989

Dolan

The Law of Letters of Credit, Commercial and Standby Credits, 2nd ed., 1991

---

1 Owing to the abundant literature, this collection is limited to books on the law of documentary credits. For further references see Schütze, *Das Dokumentenakkreditiv im Internationalen Handelsverkehr*, 5th ed., 1999, p. 361 et seq. Articles in periodicals and memorial publications are cited in the footnotes of this book.

Eichhorn
Das Dokumentenakkreditiv, 1953

Eisele
Akkreditiv und Konkurs, Diss. Tübingen 1976

Eisemann/Bontoux/Rowe
Le crédit documentaire dans le commerce extérieur, 1985

Ellinger
Documentary Letters of Credit, 1970

Eschmann
Der einstweilige Rechtsschutz des Akkreditiv-Auftraggebers in Deutschland, England und der Schweiz, 1994

Fontane
Höhere Gewalt im Dokumentenakkreditivgeschäft, 2001

Gacho
Das Akkreditiv, 1985

Gafner
Das Dokumenten-Akkreditiv nach schweizerischem Recht und dem internationalen Regulativ von 1933, Diss. Bern 1948

Gessler
Pfändungen in Akkreditive, 1967

de Gottrau
Le Crédit Documentaire et la Fraude, 1999

Gozlan
International Letters of Credit, 2nd ed., 1999

Grader van der Maas
Handbuch der Dokumenten-Akkreditive, 1963

Graffe/Weichbrodt/Xueref
Dokumenten-Akkreditive – ICC-Richtlinie 1993, 1993

Gutteridge/Megrah
The Law of Banker's Commercial Credits, 7th ed., 1984

Hahn
Die Übertragung von Dokumentenakkreditiven, Diss. Fribourg 1968

Hartmann, H.C
Die Durchsetzbarkeit des Begünstigtenanspruchs im unwiderruflichen Dokumentenakkreditiv, Diss. Tübingen 1990

Hartmann, J.
Der Akkreditiv-Eröffnungsauftrag nach den Einheitlichen Richtlinien und Gebräuchen für Dokumenten-Akkreditive (Revision 1962) und schweizerischem Recht, 1974

Hedley/Hedley
Bills of Exchange and Bankers' Documentary Credits, 4th ed., 2001

Hoeren/Florian

Rechtsfragen des internationalen Dokumentenakkreditiv und –inkasso, 1996

Horn/Freiherr von Marschall/ Rosenberg/ Pavicevic

Dokumentenakkreditive und Bankgarantien im internationalen Zahlungsverkehr, 1977

International Chamber of Commerce (ICC)

Documentary Credits Insight, quarterly newsletter since 1995

Jack

Documentary Credits, 2nd ed., 1993

Kawan

Le formalisme documentaire dans la lettre de crédit, thèse (Paris IV, Sorbonne, 1990)

Kaya

Die Grenzen der Einwendungen der Bank gegen den Zahlungsanspruch des Begünstigten aus einem unwiderruflichen Akkreditiv, 2000

Keller

L'accréditif documentaire en droit suisse, thèse (Genève, 1941)

Kilgus

'Payment of the price in international sales transactions by means of letters of credit and international bank-guarantees and the possibility of enjoying payment: a comparative study of U.S. and Swiss law; attemps by the International Chamber of Commerce (ICC) and the United Nations Commission on International Trade Law (UNCITRAL) to unify the law', 1995

Kozolchyk

'Letters of Credit', in: International Encyclopedia of Comparative Law, vol. IX, ch. 5, 1979

Kozolchyk

Commercial Letters of Credit in the Americas, 1966

Krauss

Die Konformität der Dokumente im Akkreditivgeschäft, 1990

Kurkela

Letters of credit under international trade law: UCC, UCP and Law Merchant, 1985

Loeffler

Der Einfluss des Käufer-Konkurses auf das Dokumentenakkreditivgeschäft, 1969

Lombardini

Droit et pratique du crédit documentaire, 1994

Lücke

Das Dokumentenakkreditiv in Deutschland, Frankreich und der Schweiz, Diss. Kiel 1976

Mahler
Rechtsmissbrauch und einstweiliger Rechtsschutz bei Dokumentenakkreditiven und 'Akkreditiven auf erstes Anfordern', 1986

Martinez Garcia/ Prados Martinez/Martin Lou
El credito documentario, 1970

McCullough
Letters of Credit. Commercial and Standby Letters of Credit, Bankers' and Trade Acceptances, 1997

Messerli
Das Waren- und Dokumentenakkreditiv, 2nd ed., 1975

Mukoie-Okitunungu
Le crédit documentaire, 1976

Nasser
Le crédit documentaire, 1958

Nielsen
Grundlagen des Akkreditivgeschäfts – Revision 1983, 1985

Nielsen
Dokumentenakkreditiv, in: Hellner/Steuer, Bankrecht und Bankpraxis, Looseleaf, 5/469 et seq.

Nielsen
Neue Richtlinien für Dokumenten-Akkreditive, 2nd ed., 2001

Özdamar
Rechtsfragen des Dokumentenakkreditivs in seiner Gestalt nach den ERA (Revision 1983), 1996

Poh Chu Chai
Law of Pledges, Guarantees and Letters of Credit, 4th ed., 1999

Raith
Das Recht des Dokumentenakkreditivs in den USA und in Deutschland, 1985

Richter
Standby Letter of Credit, 1990

de Rooy
Documentary Credits, 1984

Rowe
Guarantees, Standby letters of credit and other securities, 1987

Rückert
Verpflichtungen der Banken aus unwiderruflichen Dokumenten-Akkreditiven, Diss. Mainz 1960

Sambo
La tecnica del credito documentario, 1978

Sarna

Letters of Credit – The Law and Current Practice, 3rd ed., 1993

Schärrer

Die Rechtsstellung des Begünstigten im Dokuments-Akkreditiv, 1980

Schlick

Der Haftungsausschluss der Banken in bezug auf die Echtheit der Dokumente im Akkreditivgeschäft, Diss. Frankfurt/Main 1968

Schütze

Das Dokumentenakkreditiv im Internationalen Handelsverkehr, 5th ed., 1999

Slongo

Die Zahlung unter Vorbehalt im Akkreditiv-Geschäft, 1980

Stapel

Die einheitlichen Richtlinien und Gebräuche für Dokumentenakkreditive der Internationalen Handelskammer in der Fassung von 1993, 1998

Stoufflet

Le crédit documentaire, 1957 (suppl. 1958)

Taylor

Bank-to-Bank Reimbursements under Documentary Credits, 1997

Tevini du Pasquier

Le crédit documentaire en droit suisse – Droit et obligations de la banque mandataire et assignée, thèse (Genève 1990)

Theophilopoulos

The Documentary Credit, 2nd ed., 1958

Todd

Bills of Lading and Bankers' Documentary Credits, 3rd ed., 1998

Ulrich

Rechtsprobleme des Dokumentenakkreditivs, 1989

Ventris

Bankers' Documentary Credits, 2nd ed., 1983 with supp. 1985

Vidal Sola

Credito documentado irrevocable, 1958

Wassermann

Die Verwertung von Ansprüchen aus Dokumentenakkreditiven, 1981

Wiele

Das Dokumenten-Akkreditiv und der anglo-amerikanische Documentary Letter of Credit, 1955

Zahn/Eberding/Ehrlich

Zahlung und Zahlungssicherung im Aussenhandel, 6th ed. 1986, p. 35 et seq.

ICC Uniform Customs and Practice for Documentary Credits (UCP 500), 1993 revision

A. General Provisions and Definitions

Article 1

Application of UCP

The Uniform Customs and Practice for Documentary Credits, 1993 Revision, ICC Publication N°500, shall apply to all Documentary Credits (including to the extent to which they may be applicable, Standby Letter(s) of Credit) where they are incorporated into the text of the Credit. They are binding on all parties thereto, unless otherwise expressly stipulated in the Credit.

Article 2

Meaning of Credit

For the purposes of these Articles, the expressions "Documentary Credit(s)" and "Standby Letter(s) of Credit" (hereinafter referred to as "Credit(s)"), mean any arrangement, however named or described, whereby a bank (the "Issuing Bank") acting at the request and on the instructions of a customer (the "Applicant") or on its own behalf,

i. is to make a payment to or to the order of a third party (the"Beneficiary"), or is to accept and pay bills of exchange (Draft(s)) drawn by the Beneficiary,

or

ii. authorises another bank to effect such payment, or to accept and pay such bills of exchange (Draft(s)),

or

iii. authorises another bank to negotiate, against stipulated document(s),provided that the terms and conditions of the Credit are complied with.

For the purposes of these Articles, branches of a bank in different countries are considered another bank.

Article 3

Credits v. Contracts

a Credits, by their nature, are separate transactions from the sales or other contract(s) on which they may be based and banks are in no way concerned with or bound by such contract(s), even if any reference whatsoever to such contract(s) is included in the Credit. Consequently, the undertaking of a bank to pay, accept and pay Draft(s) or negotiate and/or to fulfil any other obligation under the Credit, is not subject to claims or defences by the Applicant resulting from his relationships with the Issuing Bank or the Beneficiary.

b A Beneficiary can in no case avail himself of the contractual relationships existing between the banks or between the Applicant and the Issuing Bank.

Article 4

Documents v. Goods/Services/Performances

In Credit operations all parties concerned deal with documents, and not with goods, services and/or other performances to which the documents may relate.

Article 5

Instructions to Issue/Amend Credits

a Instructions for the issuance of a Credit, the Credit itself, instructions for an amendment thereto, and the amendment itself, must be complete and precise.
In order to guard against confusion and misunderstanding, banks should discourage any attempt:
  i. to include excessive detail in the Credit or in any amendment thereto;
  ii. to give instructions to issue, advise or confirm a Credit by reference to a Credit previously issued (similar Credit) where such previous Credit has been subject to accepted amendment(s), and/or unaccepted amendment(s).

b All instructions for the issuance of a Credit and the Credit itself and, where applicable, all instructions for an amendment thereto and the amendment itself, must state precisely the document(s) against which payment, acceptance or negotiation is to be made.

B. Form and Notification of Credits

Article 6

Revocable v. Irrevocable Credits

a A Credit may be either
  i. revocable,
  or
  ii. irrevocable.

b The Credit, therefore, should clearly indicate whether it is revocable or irrevocable.

c In the absence of such indication the Credit shall be deemed to be irrevocable.

Article 7

Advising Bank's Liability

a A Credit may be advised to a Beneficiary through another bank (the "Advising Bank") without engagement on the part of the Advising Bank, but that bank, if it elects to advise the Credit, shall take reasonable care to check the apparent authenticity of the Credit which it advises. If the bank elects not to advise the Credit, it must so inform the Issuing Bank without delay.

b If the Advising Bank cannot establish such apparent authenticity it must inform, without delay, the bank from which the instructions appear to have been received that it has been unable to establish the authenticity of the Credit and if it elects nonetheless to advise the Credit it must inform the Beneficiary that it has not been able to establish the authenticity of the Credit.

Article 8

Revocation of a Credit

a A revocable Credit may be amended or cancelledby the Issuing Bank at any moment and without prior notice to the Beneficiary.

b However, the Issuing Bank must:

   i. reimburse another bank with which a revocable Credit has been made available for sight payment, acceptance or negotiation - for any payment, acceptance or negotiation made by such bank - prior to receipt by it of notice of amendment or cancellation, against documents which appear on their face to be in compliance with the terms and conditions of the Credit;

   ii. reimburse another bank with which a revocable Credit has been made available for deferred payment, if such a bank has, prior to receipt by it of notice of amendment or cancellation, taken up documents which appear on their face to be in compliance with the terms and conditions of the Credit.

Article 9

Liability of Issuing and Confirming Banks

a An irrevocable Credit constitutes a definite undertaking of the Issuing Bank, provided that the stipulated documents are presented to the Nominated Bank or to the Issuing Bank and that the terms and conditions of the Credit are complied with:

   i. if the Credit provides for sight payment - to pay at sight;

   ii. if the Credit provides for deferred payment - to pay on the maturity date(s) determinable in accordance with the stipulations of the Credit;

   iii. if the Credit provides for acceptance:

      a. by the Issuing Bank - to accept Draft(s) drawn by the Beneficiary on the Issuing Bank and pay them at maturity,

      or

      b. by another drawee bank - to accept and pay at maturity Draft(s) drawn by the Beneficiary on the Issuing Bank in the event the drawee bank stipulated in the Credit does not accept Draft(s) drawn on it, or to pay Draft(s) accepted but not paid by such drawee bank at maturity;

   iv. if the Credit provides for negotiation - to pay without recourse to drawers and/or bona fide holders, Draft(s) drawn by the Beneficiary and/or document(s) presented under the Credit. A Credit should not be issued available by Draft(s) on the Applicant. If the Credit nevertheless calls for Draft(s) on the Applicant, banks will consider such Draft(s) as an additional document(s).

b A confirmation of an irrevocable Credit by another bank (the "Confirming Bank") upon the authorisation or request of the Issuing Bank, constitutes a definite undertaking of the Confirming Bank, in addition to that of the Issuing Bank, provided that the stipulated documents are presented to the Confirming Bank or to any other Nominated Bank and that the terms and conditions of the Credit are complied with:

   i. if the Credit provides for sight payment - to pay at sight;

   ii. if the Credit provides for deferred payment- to pay on the maturity date(s) determinable in accordance with the stipulations of the Credit;

   iii. if the Credit provides for acceptance:

      a. by the Confirming Bank - to accept Draft(s) drawn by the Beneficiary on the Confirming Bank and pay them at maturity,

      or

      b. by another drawee bank - to accept and pay at maturity Draft(s) drawn by the Beneficiary on the Confirming Bank, in the event the drawee bank stipulated in the Credit does not accept Draft(s) drawn on it, or to pay Draft(s) accepted but not paid by such drawee bank at maturity;

   iv. if the Credit provides for negotiation - to negotiate without recourse to drawers and/or bona fide holders, Draft(s) drawn by the Beneficiary and/or document(s) presented under the Credit. A Credit should not be issued available by Draft(s) on the Applicant. If the Credit nevertheless calls for Draft(s) on the Applicant, banks will consider such Draft(s) as an additional document(s).

c i. If another bank is authorised or requested by the Issuing Bank to add its confirmation to a Credit but is not prepared to do so, it must so inform the Issuing Bank without delay.

ii. Unless the Issuing Bank specifies otherwise in its authorisation or request to add confirmation, the Advising Bank may advise the Credit to the Beneficiary without adding its confirmation.

d i. Except as otherwise provided by Article 48, an irrevocable Credit can neither be amended nor cancelled without the agreement of the Issuing Bank, the Confirming Bank, if any, and the Beneficiary.

ii. The Issuing Bank shall be irrevocably bound by an amendment(s) issued by it from the time of the issuance of such amendment(s). A Confirming Bank may extend its confirmation to an amendment and shall be irrevocably bound as of the time of its advice of the amendment. A Confirming Bank may, however, choose to advise an amendment to the Beneficiary without extending its confirmation and if so, must inform the Issuing Bank and the Beneficiary without delay.

iii. The terms of the original Credit (or a Credit incorporating previously accepted amendment(s)) will remain in force for the Beneficiary until the Beneficiary communicates his acceptance of the amendment to the bank that advised such amendment. The Beneficiary should give notification of acceptance or rejection of amendment(s). If the Beneficiary fails to give such notification, the tender of documents to the Nominated Bank or Issuing Bank, that conform to the Credit and to not yet accepted amendment(s), will be deemed to be notification of acceptance by the Beneficiary of such amendment(s) and as of that moment the Credit will be amended.

iv. Partial acceptance of amendments contained in one and the same advice of amendment is not allowed and consequently will not be given any effect.

Article 10

Types of Credit

a All Credits must clearly indicate whether they are available by sight payment, by deferred payment, by acceptance or by negotiation.

b i. Unless the Credit stipulates that it is available only with the Issuing Bank, all Credits must nominate the bank (the "Nominated Bank") which is authorised to pay, to incur a deferred payment undertaking, to accept Draft(s) or to negotiate. In a freely negotiable Credit, any bank is a Nominated Bank.
Presentation of documents must be made to the Issuing Bank or the Confirming Bank, if any, or any other Nominated Bank.

ii. Negotiation means the giving of value for Draft(s) and/or document(s) by the bank authorised to negotiate. Mere examination of the documents without giving of value does not constitute a negotiation.

c Unless the Nominated Bank is the Confirming Bank, nomination by the Issuing Bank does not constitute any undertaking by the Nominated Bank to pay, to incur a deferred payment undertaking, to accept Draft(s), or to negotiate. Except where expressly agreed to by the Nominated Bank and so communicated to the Beneficiary, the Nominated Bank's receipt of and/or examination and/or forwarding of the documents does not make that bank liable to pay, to incur a deferred payment undertaking, to accept Draft(s), or to negotiate.

d By nominating another bank, or by allowing for negotiation by any bank, or by authorising or requesting another bank to add its confirmation, the Issuing Bank authorises such bank to pay, accept Draft(s) or negotiate as the case may be, against documents which appear on their face to be in compliance with the terms and conditions of the Credit and undertakes to reimburse such bank in accordance with the provisions of these Articles.

Article 11

Teletransmitted and Pre-Advised Credits

a **i.** When an Issuing Bank instructs an Advising Bank by an authenticated teletransmission to advise a Credit or an amendment to a Credit, the teletransmission will be deemed to be the operative Credit instrument or the operative amendment, and no mail confirmation should be sent. Should a mail confirmation nevertheless be sent, it will have no effect and the Advising Bank will have no obligation to check such mail confirmation against the operative Credit instrument or the operative amendment received by teletransmission.

ii. If the teletransmission states "full details to follow" (or words of similar effect) or states that the mail confirmation is to be the operative Credit instrument or the operative amendment, then the teletransmission will not be deemed to be the operative Credit instrument or the operative amendment. The Issuing Bank must forward the operative Credit instrument or the operative amendment to such Advising Bank without delay.

b If a bank uses the services of an Advising Bank to have the Credit advised to the Beneficiary, it must also use the services of the same bank for advising an amendment(s).

c A preliminary advice of the issuance or amendment of an irrevocable Credit (pre-advice), shall only be given by an Issuing Bank if such bank is prepared to issue the operative Credit instrument or the operative amendment thereto. Unless otherwise stated in such preliminary advice by the Issuing Bank, an Issuing Bank having given such pre-advice shall be irrevocably committed to issue or amend the Credit, in terms not inconsistent with the pre-advice, without delay.

Article 12

Incomplete or Unclear Instructions

If incomplete or unclear instructions are received to advise, confirm or amend a Credit, the bank requested to act on such instructions may give preliminary notification to the Beneficiary for information only and without responsibility. This preliminary notification should state clearly that the notification is provided for information only and without the responsibility of the Advising Bank. In any event, the Advising Bank must inform the Issuing Bank of the action taken and request it to provide the necessary information.

The Issuing Bank must provide the necessary information without delay. The Credit will be advised, confirmed or amended, only when complete and clear instructions have been received and if the Advising Bank is then prepared to act on the instructions.

C. Liabilities and Responsibilities

Article 13

Standard for Examination of Documents

a Banks must examine all documents stipulated in the Credit with reasonable care, to ascertain whether or not they appear, on their face, to be in compliance with the terms and conditions of the Credit. Compliance of the stipulated documents on their face with the terms and conditions of the Credit, shall be determined by international standard banking practice as reflected in these Articles. Documents which appear on their face to be inconsistent with one another will be considered as not appearing on their face to be in compliance with the terms and conditions of the Credit.

Documents not stipulated in the Credit will not be examined by banks. If they receive such documents, they shall return them to the presenter or pass them on without responsibility.

b The Issuing Bank, the Confirming Bank, if any, or a Nominated Bank acting on their behalf, shall each have a reasonable time, not to exceed seven banking days following the day of receipt of the documents, to examine the documents and determine whether to take up or refuse the documents and to inform the party from which it received the documents accordingly.

c If a Credit contains conditions without stating the document(s) to be presented in compliance therewith, banks will deem such conditions as not stated and will disregard them.

Article 14

Discrepant Documents and Notice

a When the Issuing Bank authorises another bank to pay, incur a deferred payment undertaking, accept Draft(s), or negotiate against documents which appear on their face to be in compliance with the terms and conditions of the Credit, the Issuing Bank and the Confirming Bank, if any, are bound:

   i.   to reimburse the Nominated Bank which has paid, incurred a deferred payment undertaking, accepted Draft(s), or negotiated,

   ii. to take up the documents.

b Upon receipt of the documents the Issuing Bank and/or Confirming Bank, if any, or a Nominated Bank acting on their behalf, must determine on the basis of the documents alone whether or not they appear on their face to be in compliance with the terms and conditions of the Credit. If the documents appear on their face not to be in compliance with the terms and conditions of the Credit, such banks may refuse to take up the documents.

c If the Issuing Bank determines that the documents appear on their face not to be in compliance with the terms and conditions of the Credit, it may in its sole judgment approach the Applicant for a waiver of the discrepancy(ies). This does not, however, extend the period mentioned in sub-Article 13 (b).

d **i.**   If the Issuing Bank and/or Confirming Bank, if any, or a Nominated Bank acting on their behalf, decides to refuse the documents, it must give notice to that effect by telecommunication or, if that is not possible, by other expeditious means, without delay but no later than the close of the seventh banking day following the day of receipt of the documents. Such notice shall be given to the bank from which it received the documents, or to the Beneficiary, if it received the documents directly from him.

   ii. Such notice must state all discrepancies in respect of which the bank refuses the documents and must also state whether it is holding the documents at the disposal of, or is returning them to, the presenter.

   iii. The Issuing Bank and/or Confirming Bank, if any, shall then be entitled to claim from the remitting bank refund, with interest, of any reimbursement which has been made to that bank.

e If the Issuing Bank and/or Confirming Bank, if any, fails to act in accordance with the provisions of this Article and/or fails to hold the documents at the disposal of, or return them to the presenter, the Issuing Bank and/or Confirming Bank, if any, shall be precluded from claiming that the documents are not in compliance with the terms and conditions of the Credit.

f If the remitting bank draws the attention of the Issuing Bank and/or Confirming Bank, if any, to any discrepancy(ies) in the document(s) or advises such banks that it has paid, incurred a deferred payment undertaking, accepted Draft(s) or negotiated under reserve or against an indemnity in respect of such discrepancy(ies), the Issuing Bank and/or Confirming Bank, if any, shall not be thereby relieved from any of their obligations under any provision of this Article.

Such reserve or indemnity concerns only the relations between the remitting bank and the party towards whom the reserve was made, or from whom, or on whose behalf, the indemnity was obtained.

Article 15

Disclaimer on Effectiveness of Documents

Banks assume no liability or responsibility for the form, sufficiency, accuracy, genuineness, falsification or legal effect of any document(s), or for the general and/or particular conditions stipulated in the document(s) or superimposed thereon; nor do they assume any liability or responsibility for the description, quantity, weight, quality, condition, packing, delivery, value or existence of the goods represented by any document(s), or for the good faith or acts and/or omissions, solvency, performance or standing of the consignors, the carriers, the forwarders, the consignees or the insurers of the goods, or any other person whomsoever.

Article 16

Disclaimer on the Transmission of Messages

Banks assume no liability or responsibility for the consequences arising out of delay and/or loss in transit of any message(s), letter(s) or document(s), or for delay, mutilation or other error(s) arising in the transmission of any telecommunication. Banks assume no liability or responsibility for errors in translation and/or interpretation of technical terms, and reserve the right to transmit Credit terms without translating them.

Article 17

Force Majeure

Banks assume no liability or responsibility for the consequences arising out of the interruption of their business by Acts of God, riots, civil commotions, insurrections, wars or any other causes beyond their control, or by any strikes or lockouts. Unless specifically authorised, banks will not, upon resumption of their business, pay, incur a deferred payment undertaking, accept Draft(s) or negotiate under Credits which expired during such interruption of their business.

Article 18

Disclaimer for Acts of an Instructed Party

a   Banks utilizing the services of another bank or other banks for the purpose of giving effect to the instructions of the Applicant do so for the account and at the risk of such Applicant.

b   Banks assume no liability or responsibility should the instructions they transmit not be carried out, even if they have themselves taken the initiative in the choice of such other bank(s).

c   i.   A party instructing another party to perform services is liable for any charges, including commissions, fees, costs or expenses incurred by the instructed party in connection with its instructions.
    ii. Where a Credit stipulates that such charges are for the account of a party other than the instructing party, and charges cannot be collected, the instructing party remains ultimately liable for the payment thereof.

d   The Applicant shall be bound by and liable to indemnify the banks against all obligations and responsibilities imposed by foreign laws and usages.

Article 19

Bank-to-Bank Reimbursement Arrangements

a If an Issuing Bank intends that the reimbursement to which a paying, accepting or negotiating bank is entitled, shall be obtained by such bank (the "Claiming Bank"), claiming on another party (the "Reimbursing Bank"), it shall provide such Reimbursing Bank in good time with the proper instructions or authorisation to honour such reimbursement claims.

b Issuing Banks shall not require a Claiming Bank to supply a certificate of compliance with the terms and conditions of the Credit to the Reimbursing Bank.

c An Issuing Bank shall not be relieved from any of its obligations to provide reimbursement if and when reimbursement is not received by the Claiming Bank from the Reimbursing Bank.

d The Issuing Bank shall be responsible to the Claiming Bank for any loss of interest if reimbursement is not provided by the Reimbursing Bank on first demand, or as otherwise specified in the Credit, or mutually agreed, as the case may be.

e The Reimbursing Bank's charges should be for the account of the Issuing Bank. However, in cases where the charges are for the account of another party, it is the responsibility of the Issuing Bank to so indicate in the original Credit and in the reimbursement authorisation. In cases where the Reimbursing Bank's charges are for the account of another party they shall be collected from the Claiming Bank when the Credit is drawn under. In cases where the Credit is not drawn under, the Reimbursing Bank's charges remain the obligation of the Issuing Bank.

D. Documents

Article 20

Ambiguity as to the Issuers of Documents

a Terms such as "first class", "well known", "qualified", "independent", "official", "competent", "local" and the like, shall not be used to describe the issuers of any document(s) to be presented under a Credit. If such terms are incorporated in the Credit, banks will accept the relative document(s) as presented, provided that it appears on its face to be in compliance with the other terms and conditions of the Credit and not to have been issued by the Beneficiary.

b Unless otherwise stipulated in the Credit, banks will also accept as an original document(s), a document(s) produced or appearing to have been produced:
  i. by reprographic, automated or computerized systems;
  ii. as carbon copies;
  provided that it is marked as original and, where necessary, appears to be signed.
  A document may be signed by handwriting, by facsimile signature, by perforated signature, by stamp, by symbol, or by any other mechanical or electronic method of authentication.

c **i.** Unless otherwise stipulated in the Credit, banks will accept as a copy(ies), a document(s) either labelled copy or not marked as an original - a copy(ies) need not be signed.
  ii. Credits that require multiple document(s) such as "duplicate", "two fold", "two copies" and the like, will be satisfied by the presentation of one original and the remaining number in copies except where the document itself indicates otherwise.

d Unless otherwise stipulated in the Credit, a condition under a Credit calling for a document to be authenticated, validated, legalised, visaed, certified or indicating a similar requirement, will be satisfied by any signature, mark, stamp or label on such document that on its face appears to satisfy the above condition.

Article 21

Unspecified Issuers or Contents of Documents

When documents other than transport documents, insurance documents and commercial invoices are called for, the Credit should stipulate by whom such documents are to be issued and their wording or data content. If the Credit does not so stipulate, banks will accept such documents as presented, provided that their data content is not inconsistent with any other stipulated document presented.

Article 22

Issuance Date of Documents v. Credit Date

Unless otherwise stipulated in the Credit, banks will accept a document bearing a date of issuance prior to that of the Credit, subject to such document being presented within the time limits set out in the Credit and in these Articles.

Article 23

Marine/Ocean Bill of Lading

a   If a Credit calls for a bill of lading covering a port-to-port shipment, banks will, unless otherwise stipulated in the Credit, accept a document, however named, which:

i.   appears on its face to indicate the name of the carrier and to have been signed or otherwise authenticated by:
   –   the carrier or a named agent for or on behalf of the carrier, or
   –   the master or a named agent for or on behalf of the master.

Any signature or authentication of the carrier or master must be identified as carrier or master, as the case may be. An agent signing or authenticating for the carrier or master must also indicate the name and the capacity of the party, i.e. carrier or master, on whose behalf that agent is acting,

and

ii.   indicates that the goods have been loaded on board, or shipped on a named vessel.

Loading on board or shipment on a named vessel may be indicated by pre-printed wording on the bill of lading that the goods have been loaded on board a named vessel or shipped on a named vessel, in which case the date of issuance of the bill of lading will be deemed to be the date of loading on board and the date of shipment.

In all other cases loading on board a named vessel must be evidenced by a notation on the bill of lading which gives the date on which the goods have been loaded on board, in which case the date of the on board notation will be deemed to be the date of shipment.

If the bill of lading contains the indication "intended vessel", or similar qualification in relation to the vessel, loading on board a named vessel must be evidenced by an on board notation on the bill of lading which, in addition to the date on which the goods have been loaded on board, also includes the name of the vessel on which the goods have been loaded, even if they have been loaded on the vessel named as the "intended vessel".

If the bill of lading indicates a place of receipt or taking in charge different from the port of loading, the on board notation must also include the port of loading stipulated in the Credit and the name of the vessel on which the goods have been loaded, even if they have been loaded on the vessel named in the bill of lading. This provision also applies whenever loading on board the vessel is indicated by pre-printed wording on the bill of lading,

and

iii.   indicates the port of loading and the port of discharge stipulated in the Credit, notwithstanding that it:

    a.   indicates a place of taking in charge different from the port of loading, and/or a place of final destination different from the port of discharge,
        and/or

    b.   contains the indication "intended" or similar qualification in relation to the port of loading and/or port of discharge, as long as the document also states the ports of loading and/or discharge stipulated in the Credit,

and

iv.   consists of a sole original bill of lading or, if issued in more than one original, the full set as so issued,

and

v.   appears to contain all of the terms and conditions of carriage, or some of such terms and conditions by reference to a source or document other than the bill of lading (short form/blank back bill of lading); banks will not examine the contents of such terms and conditions,

and

vi.   contains no indication that it is subject to a charter party and/or no indication that the carrying vessel is propelled by sail only,

and

vii.   in all other respects meets the stipulations of the Credit.

b   For the purpose of this Article, transhipment means unloading and reloading from one vessel to another vessel during the course of ocean carriage from the port of loading to the port of discharge stipulated in the Credit.

c   Unless transhipment is prohibited by the terms of the Credit, banks will accept a bill of lading which indicates that the goods will be transhipped, provided that the entire ocean carriage is covered by one and the same bill of lading.

d   Even if the Credit prohibits transhipment, banks will accept a bill of lading which:

i.   indicates that transhipment will take place as long as the relevant cargo is shipped in Container(s), Trailer(s) and/or "LASH" barge(s) as evidenced by the bill of lading, provided that the entire ocean carriage is covered by one and the same bill of lading,
and/or

ii.   incorporates clauses stating that the carrier reserves the right to tranship.

Article 24

Non-Negotiable Sea Waybill

a   If a Credit calls for a non-negotiable sea waybill covering a port-to-port shipment, banks will, unless otherwise stipulated in the Credit, accept a document, however named, which:

i.   appears on its face to indicate the name of the carrier and to have been signed or otherwise authenticated by:

–   the carrier or a named agent for or on behalf of the carrier, or
–   the master or a named agent for or on behalf of the master,

Any signature or authentication of the carrier or master must be identified as carrier or master, as the case may be. An agent signing or authenticating for the carrier or master must also indicate the name and the capacity of the party, i.e. carrier or master, on whose behalf that agent is acting,

and

ii.   indicates that the goods have been loaded on board, or shipped on a named vessel. Loading on board or shipment on a named vessel may be indicated by pre-printed wording on the non-negotiable sea waybill that the goods have been loaded on board a named vessel or shipped on a named vessel, in which case the date of issuance of the non-negotiable sea waybill will be deemed to be the date of loading on board and the date of shipment.

In all other cases loading on board a named vessel must be evidenced by a notation on the non-negotiable sea waybill which gives the date on which the goods have been loaded on board, in which case the date of the on board notation will be deemed to be the date of shipment.

If the non-negotiable sea waybill contains the indication "intended vessel", or similar qualification in relation to the vessel, loading on board a named vessel must be evidenced by an on board notation on the non-negotiable sea waybill which, in addition to the date on which the goods have been loaded on board, includes the name of the vessel on which the goods have been loaded, even if they have been loaded on the vessel named as the "intended vessel".

If the non-negotiable sea waybill indicates a place of receipt or taking in charge different from the port of loading, the on board notation must also include the port of loading stipulated in the Credit and the name of the vessel on which the goods have been loaded, even if they have been loaded on a vessel named in the non-negotiable sea waybill. This provision also applies whenever loading on board the vessel is indicated by pre-printed wording on the non-negotiable sea waybill,

and

iii. indicates the port of loading and the port of discharge stipulated in the Credit, notwithstanding that it:

    a. indicates a place of taking in charge different from the port of loading, and/or a place of final destination different from the port of discharge,

    and/or

    b. contains the indication "intended" or similar qualification in relation to the port of loading and/or port of discharge, as long as the document also states the ports of loading and/or discharge stipulated in the Credit,

and

iv. consists of a sole original non-negotiable sea waybill, or if issued in more than one original, the full set as so issued,

and

v. appears to contain all of the terms and conditions of carriage, or some of such terms and conditions by reference to a source or document other than the non-negotiable sea waybill (short form/blank back non-negotiable sea waybill); banks will not examine the contents of such terms and conditions,

and

vi. contains no indication that it is subject to a charter party and/or no indication that the carrying vessel is propelled by sail only,

and

vii. in all other respects meets the stipulations of the Credit.

b For the purpose of this Article, transhipment means unloading and reloading from one vessel to another vessel during the course of ocean carriage from the port of loading to the port of discharge stipulated in the Credit.

c Unless transhipment is prohibited by the terms of the Credit, banks will accept a non-negotiable sea waybill which indicates that the goods will be transhipped, provided that the entire ocean carriage is covered by one and the same non-negotiable sea waybill.

d Even if the Credit prohibits transhipment, banks will accept a non-negotiable sea waybill which:

    i. indicates that transhipment will take place as long as the relevant cargo is shipped in Container(s), Trailer(s) and/or "LASH" barge(s) as evidenced by the non-negotiable sea waybill, provided that the entire ocean carriage is covered by one and the same non-negotiable sea waybill,

    and/or

    ii. incorporates clauses stating that the carrier reserves the right to tranship.

Article 25
Charter Party Bill of Lading

a If a Credit calls for or permits a charter party bill of lading, banks will, unless otherwise stipulated in the Credit, accept a document, however named, which:

i. contains any indication that it is subject to a charter party,

and

ii. appears on its face to have been signed or otherwise authenticated by:
- the master or a named agent for or on behalf of the master, or
- the owner or a named agent for or on behalf of the owner.

Any signature or authentication of the master or owner must be identified as master or owner as the case may be. An agent signing or authen-ticating for the master or owner must also indicate the name and the capacity of the party, i.e. master or owner, on whose behalf that agent is acting,

and

iii. does or does not indicate the name of the carrier,

and

iv. indicates that the goods have been loaded on board or shipped on a named vessel.

Loading on board or shipment on a named vessel may be indicated by pre-printed wording on the bill of lading that the goods have been loaded on board a named vessel or shipped on a named vessel, in which case the date of issuance of the bill of lading will be deemed to be the date of loading on board and the date of shipment.

In all other cases loading on board a named vessel must be evidenced by a notation on the bill of lading which gives the date on which the goods have been loaded on board, in which case the date of the on board notation will be deemed to be the date of shipment,

and

v. indicates the port of loading and the port of discharge stipulated in the Credit,

and

vi. consists of a sole original bill of lading or, if issued in more than one original, the full set as so issued,

and

vii. contains no indication that the carrying vessel is propelled by sail only,

and

viii. in all other respects meets the stipulations of the Credit.

b Even if the Credit requires the presentation of a charter party contract in connection with a charter party bill of lading, banks will not examine such charter party contract, but will pass it on without responsibility on their part.

Article 26
Multimodal Transport Document

a If a Credit calls for a transport document covering at least two different modes of transport (multimodal transport), banks will, unless otherwise stipulated in the Credit, accept a document, however named, which:

i. appears on its face to indicate the name of the carrier or multimodal transport operator and to have been signed or otherwise authenticated by:
- the carrier or multimodal transport operator or a named agent for or on behalf of the carrier or multimodal transport operator, or
- the master or a named agent for or on behalf of the master.

Any signature or authentication of the carrier, multimodal transport operator or master must be identified as carrier, multimodal transport operator or master, as the case may be. An agent signing or authenticating for the carrier, multimodal transport operator or master must also indicate the name and the capacity of the party, i.e. carrier, multimodal transport operator or master, on whose behalf that agent is act-ing,

and

ii. indicates that the goods have been dispatched, taken in charge or loaded on board. Dispatch, taking in charge or loading on board may be indicated by wording to that effect on the multimodal transport document and the date of issuance will be deemed to be the date of dispatch, taking in charge or loading on board and the date of shipment. However, if the document indicates, by stamp or otherwise, a date of dispatch, taking in charge or loading on board, such date will be deemed to be the date of shipment,

and

iii. a. indicates the place of taking in charge stipulated in the Credit which may be different from the port, airport or place of loading, and the place of final destination stipulated in the Credit which may be different from the port, airport or place of discharge,

and/or

b. contains the indication "intended" or similar qualification in relation to the vessel and/or port of loading and/or port of discharge,

and

iv. consists of a sole original multimodal transport document or, if issued in more than one original, the full set as so issued,

and

v. appears to contain all of the terms and conditions of carriage, or some of such terms and conditions by reference to a source or document other than the multimodal transport document (short form/blank back multimodal transport document); banks will not examine the contents of such terms and conditions,

and

vi. contains no indication that it is subject to a charter party and/or no indication that the carrying vessel is propelled by sail only,

and

vii. in all other respects meets the stipulations of the Credit.

b Even if the Credit prohibits transhipment, banks will accept a multimodal transport document which indicates that transhipment will or may take place, provided that the entire carriage is covered by one and the same multimodal transport document.

Article 27

Air Transport Document

a If a Credit calls for an air transport document, banks will, unless otherwise stipulated in the Credit, accept a document, however named, which:

i. appears on its face to indicate the name of the carrier and to have been signed or otherwise authenticated by:

- the carrier, or
- a named agent for or on behalf of the carrier.

Any signature or authentication of the carrier must be identified as carrier. An agent signing or authenticating for the carrier must also indicate the name and the capacity of the party, i.e. carrier, on whose behalf that agent is acting,

and

ii. indicates that the goods have been accepted for carriage,

and

iii. where the Credit calls for an actual date of dispatch, indicates a specific notation of such date, the date of dispatch so indicated on the air transport document will be deemed to be the date of shipment.

For the purpose of this Article, the information appearing in the box on the air transport document (marked "For Carrier Use Only" or similar expression) relative to the flight number and date will not be considered as a specific notation of such date of dispatch.

In all other cases, the date of issuance of the air transport document will be deemed to be the date of shipment,

and

iv. indicates the airport of departure and the airport of destination stipulated in the Credit,

and

v. appears to be the original for consignor/shipper even if the Credit stipulates a full set of originals, or similar expressions,

and

vi. appears to contain all of the terms and conditions of carriage, or some of such terms and conditions, by reference to a source or document other than the air transport document; banks will not examine the contents of such terms and conditions,

and

vii. in all other respects meets the stipulations of the Credit.

b For the purpose of this Article, transhipment means unloading and reloading from one aircraft to another aircraft during the course of carriage from the airport of departure to the airport of destination stipulated in the Credit.

c Even if the Credit prohibits transhipment, banks will accept an air transport document which indicates that transhipment will or may take place, provided that the entire carriage is covered by one and the same air transport document.

Article 28
Road, Rail or Inland Waterway Transport Documents

a If a Credit calls for a road, rail, or inland waterway transport document, banks will, unless otherwise stipulated in the Credit, accept a document of the type called for, however named, which:

i. appears on its face to indicate the name of the carrier and to have been signed or otherwise authenticated by the carrier or a named agent for or on behalf of the carrier and/or to bear a reception stamp or other indication of receipt by the carrier or a named agent for or on behalf of the carrier.

Any signature, authentication, reception stamp or other indication of receipt of the carrier, must be identified on its face as that of the carrier. An agent signing or authenticating for the carrier, must also indicate the name and the capacity of the party, i.e. carrier, on whose behalf that agent is acting,

and

ii. indicates that the goods have been received for shipment, dispatch or carriage or wording to this effect. The date of issuance will be deemed to be the date of shipment unless the transport document contains a reception stamp, in which case the date of the reception stamp will be deemed to be the date of shipment,

and

iii. indicates the place of shipment and the place of destination stipulated in the Credit,

and

iv. in all other respects meets the stipulations of the Credit.

b   In the absence of any indication on the transport document as to the numbers issued, banks will accept the transport document(s) presented as constituting a full set. Banks will accept as original(s) the transport document(s) whether marked as original(s) or not.

c   For the purpose of this Article, transhipment means unloading and reloading from one means of conveyance to another means of conveyance, in different modes of transport, during the course of carriage from the place of shipment to the place of destination stipulated in the Credit.

d   Even if the Credit prohibits transhipment, banks will accept a road, rail, or inland waterway transport document which indicates that transhipment will or may take place, provided that the entire carriage is covered by one and the same transport document and within the same mode of transport.

Article 29

Courier and Post Receipts

a   If a Credit calls for a post receipt or certificate of posting, banks will, unless otherwise stipulated in the Credit, accept a post receipt or certificate of posting which:

   i.   appears on its face to have been stamped or otherwise authenticated and dated in the place from which the Credit stipulates the goods are to be shipped or dispatched and such date will be deemed to be the date of shipment or dispatch,

   and

   ii.   in all other respects meets the stipulations of the Credit.

b   If a Credit calls for a document issued by a courier or expedited delivery service evidencing receipt of the goods for delivery, banks will, unless otherwise stipulated in the Credit, accept a document, however named, which:

   i.   appears on its face to indicate the name of the courier/service, and to have been stamped, signed or otherwise authenticated by such named courier/service (unless the Credit specifically calls for a document issued by a named Courier/Service, banks will accept a document issued by any Courier/Service),

   and

   ii.   indicates a date of pick-up or of receipt or wording to this effect, such date being deemed to be the date of shipment or dispatch,

   and

   iii.   in all other respects meets the stipulations of the Credit.

Article 30

Transport Documents issued by Freight Forwarders

Unless otherwise authorised in the Credit, banks will only accept a transport document issued by a freight forwarder if it appears on its face to indicate:

   i.   the name of the freight forwarder as a carrier or multimodal transport operator and to have been signed or otherwise authenticated by the freight forwarder as carrier or multimodal transport operator,

or

   ii.   the name of the carrier or multimodal transport operator and to have been signed or otherwise authenticated by the freight forwarder as a named agent for or on behalf of the carrier or multimodal transport operator.

Article 31

On Deck, Shipper's Load and Count, Name of Consignor

Unless otherwise stipulated in the Credit, banks will accept a transport document which:

i. does not indicate, in the case of carriage by sea or by more than one means of conveyance including carriage by sea, that the goods are or will be loaded on deck. Nevertheless, banks will accept a transport document which contains a provision that the goods may be carried on deck, provided that it does not specifically state that they are or will be loaded on deck,

and/or

ii. bears a clause on the face thereof such as "shipper's load and count" or "said by shipper to contain" or words of similar effect,

and/or

iii. indicates as the consignor of the goods a party other than the Beneficiary of the Credit.

Article 32

Clean Transport Documents

a A clean transport document is one which bears no clause or notation which expressly declares a defective condition of the goods and/or the packaging.

b Banks will not accept transport documents bearing such clauses or notations unless the Credit expressly stipulates the clauses or notations which may be accepted.

c Banks will regard a requirement in a Credit for a transport document to bear the clause "clean on board" as complied with if such transport document meets the requirements of this Article and of Articles 23, 24, 25, 26, 27, 28 or 30.

Article 33

Freight Payable/Prepaid Transport Documents

a Unless otherwise stipulated in the Credit, or inconsistent with any of the documents presented under the Credit, banks will accept transport documents stating that freight or transportation charges (hereafter referred to as "freight") have still to be paid.

b If a Credit stipulates that the transport document has to indicate that freight has been paid or prepaid, banks will accept a transport document on which words clearly indicating payment or prepayment of freight appear by stamp or otherwise, or on which payment or prepayment of freight is indicated by other means. If the Credit requires courier charges to be paid or prepaid banks will also accept a transport document issued by a courier or expedited delivery service evidencing that courier charges are for the account of a party other than the consignee.

c The words "freight prepayable" or "freight to be prepaid" or words of similar effect, if appearing on transport documents, will not be accepted as constituting evidence of the payment of freight.

d Banks will accept transport documents bearing reference by stamp or otherwise to costs additional to the freight, such as costs of, or disbursements incurred in connection with, loading, unloading or similar operations, unless the conditions of the Credit specifically prohibit such reference.

Article 34

Insurance Documents

a Insurance documents must appear on their face to be issued and signed by insurance companies or underwriters or their agents.

b If the insurance document indicates that it has been issued in more than one original, all the originals must be presented unless otherwise authorised in the Credit.

c Cover notes issued by brokers will not be accepted, unless specifically authorised in the Credit.

d   Unless otherwise stipulated in the Credit, banks will accept an insurance certificate or a declaration under an open cover pre-signed by insurance companies or underwriters or their agents. If a Credit specifically calls for an insurance certificate or a declaration under an open cover, banks will accept, in lieu thereof, an insurance policy.

e   Unless otherwise stipulated in the Credit, or unless it appears from the insurance document that the cover is effective at the latest from the date of loading on board or dispatch or taking in charge of the goods, banks will not accept an insurance document which bears a date of issuance later than the date of loading on board or dispatch or taking in charge as indicated in such transport document.

f   i.   Unless otherwise stipulated in the Credit, the insurance document must be expressed in the same currency as the Credit.

ii.   Unless otherwise stipulated in the Credit, the minimum amount for which the insurance document must indicate the insurance cover to have been effected is the CIF (cost, insurance and freight (… "named port of destination")) or CIP (carriage and insurance paid to (…"named place of destination")) value of the goods, as the case may be, plus 10%, but only when the CIF or CIP value can be determined from the documents on their face. Otherwise, banks will accept as such minimum amount 110% of the amount for which payment, acceptance or negotiation is requested under the Credit, or 110% of the gross amount of the invoice, whichever is the greater.

Article 35

Type of Insurance Cover

a   Credits should stipulate the type of insurance required and, if any, the additional risks which are to be covered. Imprecise terms such as "usual risks" or "customary risks" shall not be used; if they are used, banks will accept insurance documents as presented, without responsibility for any risks not being covered.

b   Failing specific stipulations in the Credit, banks will accept insurance documents as presented, without responsibility for any risks not being covered.

c   Unless otherwise stipulated in the Credit, banks will accept an insurance document which indicates that the cover is subject to a franchise or an excess (deductible).

Article 36

All Risks Insurance Cover

Where a Credit stipulates "insurance against all risks", banks will accept an insurance document which contains any "all risks" notation or clause, whether or not bearing the heading "all risks", even if the insurance document indicates that certain risks are excluded, without responsibility for any risk(s) not being covered.

Article 37

Commercial Invoices

a   Unless otherwise stipulated in the Credit, commercial invoices;

i.   must appear on their face to be issued by the Beneficiary named in the Credit (except as provided in Article 48),
and

ii.   must be made out in the name of the Applicant (except as provided in sub-Article 48 (h)),
and

iii.   need not be signed.

b Unless otherwise stipulated in the Credit, banks may refuse commercial invoices issued for amounts in excess of the amount permitted by the Credit. Nevertheless, if a bank authorised to pay, incur a deferred payment undertaking, accept Draft(s), or negotiate under a Credit accepts such invoices, its decision will be binding upon all parties, provided that such bank has not paid, incurred a deferred payment undertaking, accepted Draft(s) or negotiated for an amount in excess of that permitted by the Credit.

c The description of the goods in the commercial invoice must correspond with the description in the Credit. In all other documents, the goods may be described in general terms not inconsistent with the description of the goods in the Credit.

Article 38

Other Documents

If a Credit calls for an attestation or certification of weight in the case of transport other than by sea, banks will accept a weight stamp or declaration of weight which appears to have been superimposed on the transport document by the carrier or his agent unless the Credit specifically stipulates that the attestation or certification of weight must be by means of a separate document.

E. Miscellaneous Provisions

Article 39

Allowances in Credit Amount, Quantity and Unit Price

a The words "about", "approximately", "circa" or similar expressions used in connection with the amount of the Credit or the quantity or the unit price stated in the Credit are to be construed as allowing a difference not to exceed 10% more or 10% less than the amount or the quantity or the unit price to which they refer.

b Unless a Credit stipulates that the quantity of the goods specified must not be exceeded or reduced, a tolerance of 5% more or 5% less will be permissible, always provided that the amount of the drawings does not exceed the amount of the Credit. This tolerance does not apply when the Credit stipulates the quantity in terms of a stated number of packing units or individual items.

c Unless a Credit which prohibits partial shipments stipulates otherwise, or unless sub-Article (b) above is applicable, a tolerance of 5% less in the amount of the drawing will be permissible, provided that if the Credit stipulates the quantity of the goods, such quantity of goods is shipped in full, and if the Credit stipulates a unit price, such price is not reduced. This provision does not apply when expressions referred to in sub-Article (a) above are used in the Credit.

Article 40

Partial Shipments/Drawings

a Partial drawings and/or shipments are allowed, unless the Credit stipulates otherwise.

b Transport documents which appear on their face to indicate that shipment has been made on the same means of conveyance and for the same journey, provided they indicate the same destination, will not be regarded as covering partial shipments, even if the transport documents indicate different dates of shipment and/or different ports of loading, places of taking in charge, or despatch.

c Shipments made by post or by courier will not be regarded as partial shipments if the post receipts or certificates of posting or courier's receipts or dispatch notes appear to have been stamped, signed or otherwise authenticated in the place from which the Credit stipulates the goods are to be dispatched, and on the same date.

Article 41

Instalment Shipments/Drawings

If drawings and/or shipments by instalments within given periods are stipulated in the Credit and any instalment is not drawn and/or shipped within the period allowed for that instalment, the Credit ceases to be available for that and any subsequent instalments, unless otherwise stipulated in the Credit.

Article 42

Expiry Date and Place for Presentation of Documents

a All Credits must stipulate an expiry date and a place for presentation of documents for payment, acceptance, or with the exception of freely negotiable Credits, a place for presentation of documents for negotiation. An expiry date stipulated for payment, acceptance or negotiation will be construed to express an expiry date for presentation of documents.

b Except as provided in sub-Article 44(a), documents must be presented on or before such expiry date.

c If an Issuing Bank states that the Credit is to be available "for one month", "for six months", or the like, but does not specify the date from which the time is to run, the date of issuance of the Credit by the Issuing Bank will be deemed to be the first day from which such time is to run. Banks should discourage indication of the expiry date of the Credit in this manner.

Article 43

Limitation on the Expiry Date

a In addition to stipulating an expiry date for presentation of documents, every Credit which calls for a transport document(s) should also stipulate a specified period of time after the date of shipment during which presentation must be made in compliance with the terms and conditions of the Credit. If no such period of time is stipulated, banks will not accept documents presented to them later than 21 days after the date of shipment. In any event, documents must be presented not later than the expiry date of the Credit.

b In cases in which sub-Article 40(b) applies, the date of shipment will be considered to be the latest shipment date on any of the transport documents presented.

Article 44

Extension of Expiry Date

a If the expiry date of the Credit and/or the last day of the period of time for presentation of documents stipulated by the Credit or applicable by virtue of Article 43 falls on a day on which the bank to which presentation has to be made is closed for reasons other than those referred to in Article 17, the stipulated expiry date and/or the last day of the period of time after the date of shipment for presentation of documents, as the case may be, shall be extended to the first following day on which such bank is open.

b   The latest date for shipment shall not be extended by reason of the extension of the expiry date and/or the period of time after the date of shipment for presentation of documents in accordance with sub-Article (a) above. If no such latest date for shipment is stipulated in the Credit or amendments thereto, banks will not accept transport documents indicating a date of shipment later than the expiry date stipulated in the Credit or amendments thereto.

c   The bank to which presentation is made on such first following business day must provide a statement that the documents were presented within the time limits extended in accordance with sub-Article 44(a) of the Uniform Customs and Practice for Documentary Credits, 1993 Revision, ICC Publication No. 500.

Article 45

Hours of Presentation

Banks are under no obligation to accept presentation of documents outside their banking hours.

Article 46

General Expressions as to Dates for Shipment

a   Unless otherwise stipulated in the Credit, the expression "shipment" used in stipulating an earliest and/or a latest date for shipment will be understood to include expressions such as, "loading on board", "dispatch", "accepted for carriage", "date of post receipt", "date of pick-up", and the like, and in the case of a Credit calling for a multimodal transport document the expression "taking in charge".

b   Expressions such as "prompt", "immediately", "as soon as possible", and the like should not be used. If they are used banks will disregard them.

c   If the expression "on or about" or similar expressions are used, banks will interpret them as a stipulation that shipment is to be made during the period from five days before to five days after the specified date, both end days included.

Article 47

Date Terminology for Periods of Shipment

a   The words "to", "until", "till", "from" and words of similar import applying to any date or period in the Credit referring to shipment will be understood to include the date mentioned.

b   The word "after" will be understood to exclude the date mentioned.

c   The terms "first half", "second half" of a month shall be construed respectively as the 1st to the 15th, and the 16th to the last day of such month, all dates inclusive.

d   The terms "beginning", "middle", or "end" of a month shall be construed respectively as the 1st to the 10th, the 11th to the 20th, and the 21st to the last day of such month, all dates inclusive.

F. Transferable Credit

Article 48

Transferable Credit

a   A transferable Credit is a Credit under which the Beneficiary (First Beneficiary) may request the bank authorised to pay, incur a deferred payment undertaking, accept or negotiate (the

"Transferring Bank"), or in the case of a freely negotiable Credit, the bank specifically authorised in the Credit as a Transferring Bank, to make the Credit available in whole or in part to one or more other Beneficiary(ies) (Second Beneficiary(ies)).

b A Credit can be transferred only if it is expressly designated as "transferable" by the Issuing Bank. Terms such as "divisible", "fractionable", "assignable", and "transmissible" do not render the Credit transferable. If such terms are used they shall be disregarded.

c The Transferring Bank shall be under no obligation to effect such transfer except to the extent and in the manner expressly consented to by such bank.

d At the time of making a request for transfer and prior to transfer of the Credit, the First Beneficiary must irrevocably instruct the Transferring Bank whether or not he retains the right to refuse to allow the Transferring Bank to advise amendments to the Second Beneficiary(ies). If the Transferring Bank consents to the transfer under these conditions, it must, at the time of transfer, advise the Second Beneficiary(ies) of the First Beneficiary's instructions regarding amendments.

e If a Credit is transferred to more than one Second Beneficiary(ies), refusal of an amendment by one or more Second Beneficiary(ies) does not invalidate the acceptance(s) by the other Second Bene-ficiary(ies) with respect to whom the Credit will be amended accordingly. With respect to the Second Beneficiary(ies) who rejected the amendment, the Credit will remain unamended.

f Transferring Bank charges in respect of transfers including commissions, fees, costs or expenses are payable by the First Beneficiary, unless otherwise agreed. If the Transferring Bank agrees to transfer the Credit it shall be under no obligation to effect the transfer until such charges are paid.

g Unless otherwise stated in the Credit, a transferable Credit can be transferred once only. Consequently, the Credit cannot be transferred at the request of the Second Beneficiary to any subsequent Third Beneficiary. For the purpose of this Article, a retransfer to the First Beneficiary does not constitute a prohibited transfer.

Fractions of a transferable Credit (not exceeding in the aggregate the amount of the Credit) can be transferred separately, provided partial shipments/drawings are not prohibited, and the aggregate of such transfers will be considered as constituting only one transfer of the Credit.

h The Credit can be transferred only on the terms and conditions specified in the original Credit, with the exception of:
- the amount of the Credit,
- any unit price stated therein,
- the expiry date,
- the last date for presentation of documents in accordance with Article 43,
- the period for shipment,
any or all of which may be reduced or curtailed.

The percentage for which insurance cover must be effected may be increased in such a way as to provide the amount of cover stipulated in the original Credit, or these Articles.

In addition, the name of the First Beneficiary can be substituted for that of the Applicant, but if the name of the Applicant is specifically required by the original Credit to appear in any document(s) other than the invoice, such requirement must be fulfilled.

i   The First Beneficiary has the right to substitute his own invoice(s) (and Draft(s)) for those of the Second Beneficiary(ies), for amounts not in excess of the original amount stipulated in the Credit and for the original unit prices if stipulated in the Credit, and upon such substitution of invoice(s) (and Draft(s)) the First Beneficiary can draw under the Credit for the difference, if any, between his invoice(s) and the Second Beneficiary's(ies') invoice(s).

When a Credit has been transferred and the First Beneficiary is to supply his own invoice(s) (and Draft(s)) in exchange for the Second Bene-ficiary's(ies') invoice(s) (and Draft(s)) but fails to do so on first demand, the Transferring Bank has the right to deliver to the Issuing Bank the documents received under the transferred Credit, including the Second Beneficiary's(ies') invoice(s) (and Draft(s)) without further responsibility to the First Beneficiary.

j   The First Beneficiary may request that payment or negotiation be effected to the Second Beneficiary(ies) at the place to which the Credit has been transferred up to and including the expiry date of the Credit, unless the original Credit expressly states that it may not be made available for payment or negotiation at a place other than that stipulated in the Credit. This is without prejudice to the First Beneficiary's right to substitute subsequently his own invoice(s) (and Draft(s)) for those of the Second Beneficiary(ies) and to claim any difference due to him.

G. Assignment of Proceeds

Article 49

Assignment of Proceeds

The fact that a Credit is not stated to be transferable shall not affect the Beneficiary's right to assign any proceeds to which he may be, or may become, entitled under such Credit, in accordance with the provisions of the applicable law. This Article relates only to the assignment of proceeds and not to the assignment of the right to perform under the Credit itself.

ICC at a glance

ICC is the world business organization. It is the only representative body that speaks with authority on behalf of enterprises from all sectors in every part of the world.

ICC's purpose is to promote an open international trade and investment system and the market economy worldwide. It makes rules that govern the conduct of business across borders. It provides essential services, foremost among them the ICC International Court of Arbitration, the world's leading institution of its kind.

Within a year of the creation of the United Nations, ICC was granted consultative status at the highest level with the UN and its specialized agencies. Today ICC is the preferred partner of international and regional organizations whenever decisions have to be made on global issues of importance to business.

Business leaders and experts drawn from ICC membership establish the business stance on broad issues of trade and investment policy as well as on vital technical or sectoral subjects. These include financial services, information technologies, telecommunications, marketing ethics, the environment, transportation, competition law and intellectual property, among others.

ICC was founded in 1919 by a handful of far-sighted business leaders. Today it groups thousands of member companies and associations from over 130 countries. National committees in all major capitals coordinate with their membership to address the concerns of the business community and to put across to their governments the business views formulated by ICC.

Some ICC Services

The ICC International Court of Arbitration (Paris)
The ICC International Centre for Expertise (Paris)
The ICC World Chambers Federation (Paris)
The ICC Institute of World Business Law (Paris)
The ICC Centre for Maritime Co-operation (London)
ICC Commercial Crime Services (London), grouping:
The ICC Counterfeiting Intelligence Bureau
The ICC Commercial Crime Bureau
The ICC International Maritime Bureau

Selected ICC Publications

*E: English – F: French – D: German – S: Spanish – EF: English/French bilingual edition –
E-F: separate edition in each language*

DOCUMENTARY CREDITS

Opinions of the ICC Banking Commission 1998–1999
Queries and responses on UCP 500, UCP 400 and URC 522
Edited by Gary Collyer
The third volume in a series of ICC Banking Commission Opinions interpreting
UCP 500, ICC's universally used rules on letters of credit. Containing more than
80 Opinions, this valuable reference work will serve as a guide to bankers, traders,
practitioners and the courts as to how UCP 500 should be applied on a daily basis.

E   140 pages   ISBN 92.842.1268.5   No. 613

More Queries and Responses on UCP 500 – Opinions of the ICC
Banking Commission 1997
These official responses to over 50 queries have helped practitioners and courts
correctly interpret UCP 500 – the universally accepted code of practice on letters
of credit. Includes a consolidated index, covering this and the preceding volume.

E   92 pages   ISBN 92-842-1253-7   No. 596

Documentary Credits Insight
This ICC newsletter, published four times a year, keeps the reader updated on
developments worldwide which impact directly on his or her business. ICC experts
analyze how the UCP 500 is implemented in everyday situations, and there are
national updates on documentary credit developments from correspondents in
more than thirty countries. Along with hard-hitting interviews and all the latest
L/C news, this valuable newsletter provides the text of important court decisions
concerning the UCP and a calendar of seminars, conferences and other events.

E   Periodical/subscription   4 issues a year

DC-PRO Focus
A website developed by ICC providing bankers and traders with information
relative to documentary credits. No more leafing through reams of documents
to find the L/C information needed. DC-PRO Focus puts it all on your screen for
immediate access.

More information on ICC's web site at **www.iccwbo.org.**

BANKING AND FINANCE

Bank Guarantees in International Trade

by R. Bertrams. A co-publication ICC Publishing/Kluwer Law International
This fully revised second edition serves to broaden the understanding of bank guarantees, emphasizing the implications and issues which can arise in the daily functioning of these legal instruments. Written from a transnational perspective, the book has been updated and amended in the light of new developments in the law and changing patterns in practice, and accounts for the introduction of new techniques and problem areas.
E   450 pages   ISBN 92-842-1198-0   No. 547

A User's Handbook to the Uniform Rules for Demand Guarantees (URDG)

by Dr Georges Affaki
A clear and comprehensive guide that provides a masterly presentation of the rules within the context of day-to-day bank operations. The book covers the issuance, drafting, advantages and history of the rules and explodes a number of myths that have hindered more widespread adoption of the URDG. Complete with an index to the URDG Articles, as well as a general index, this practical handbook is destined to become the essential companion to all users of the URDG.
E   208 pages   ISBN 92-842-1294-4   No. 631

Investing and Trading in Emerging Markets

by Nick Douch
Written by an emerging market strategist and risk adviser, this book highlights the risks and reveals the opportunities to be had in investing in emerging markets. With an emphasis on maintaining a structured approach, the author looks at investors' motivation, explains the importance of exchange rate regimes, and looks at the exposures faced by companies importing and exporting to emerging markets. It examines how the risks that these exposures cause can be reduced or how their negative effects can be protected against. An invaluable primer that will be returned to again and again as new opportunities or risks present themselves.
E   104 pages   ISBN 92-842-1240-5   No. 582

Bills of Exchange (third edition)

by Dr jur. Uwe Jahn

Now in its third edition, this fully revised publication has been expanded to cover legislation in Europe, Asia and Oceania. Designed for easy reference, the clear text provides a comprehensive comparison of bills of exchange law in 67 countries and offers practical information on everyday problems in overcoming conflicts in national laws. Dr Uwe Jahn is an acknowledged expert in the field and author of a number of books on international commercial law.

E   192 pages   ISBN 92-842-1250-2   No. 593

HOW TO OBTAIN ICC PUBLICATIONS

ICC Publications are available from ICC national committees or councils which exist in nearly 80 countries or from:

ICC PUBLISHING S.A.
38, Cours Albert 1er
75008 Paris – France
Customer Service:
Tel: +33 1 49 53 29 23/28 89
Fax: +33 1 49 53 29 02
e-mail: pub@iccwbo.org

ICC PUBLISHING, INC.
156 Fifth Avenue, Suite 417
New York, NY 10010
USA
Tel: +1 (212) 206 1150
Fax: +1 (212) 633 6025
e-mail: info@iccpub.net

To find out more about the latest ICC publications, visit our website at
www.iccbooks.com